Jazz Bea

More Notes on Classic Jazz

By Lew Shaw

AZtold Publishing
Scottsdale, Arizona

JAZZ BEAT ENCORE
More Notes on Classic Jazz Lew Shaw

Shaw, Lew
Jazz Beat Encore-More Notes on Classic Jazz/Lew Shaw

ISBN
979-8-6272656-7-4

**For updates or questions,
contact: azscribe@wmvaz.com**

Published in the United States of America

TABLE OF CONTENTS

PRELUDE

A sage once said if music could be put into words, we wouldn't need music. Still, it's good that over the years, there have been people willing to write about it. We have no recordings of, say, Beethoven. However, we do have articulately-written accounts of his playing and his persona, for which we should be thankful. With regard to jazz, many people want to know something about the man or woman behind the horn (or seated on the piano stool). This is where people like Otis Ferguson, Eddie Condon, Whitney Balliett, Stanley Dance and Lew Shaw come in.

Lew has been writing those kinds of "articulate accounts" for many years. Like Condon and Dance before him, Lew wisely lets the musicians do most of the talking. Many musicians let their music speak for them, but just as many have a lot to say when they get off the bandstand!

It helps when musicians know they are talking with someone who understands their quirky lifestyle and their different ways of seeing the world. I know that I do. Lew has a perceptive ear. In **JAZZ BEAT ENCORE**, you'll find he has a savvy way of presenting these 43 musicians' stories in a way that helps us learn just what makes a jazz musician tick. *Or tock.*

I'm confident you'll enjoy Lew Shaw's latest offering of *"More Notes on Classic Jazz.".* Now please turn the page.

Dan Barrett
Costa Mesa, California

APPLAUSE

Writing and publishing a book is never a solo effort. I am particularly indebted to:

My "musical consultant" Ed Polcer whose prodding convinced me to publish my first book about musicians who play Classic Jazz and who has continued to be a source of counsel and support;

The musicians and individuals who gave of their time to share their thoughts that provided the substance of this book; and the photographers whose images visualize the individuals profiled;

My former ad agency colleague Bill Withrow who came through with another award-winning cover design; and Marty Faulkner who has guided me through some of the more technical aspects of producing an eBook and digital paperback;

Jeff Keane, for allowing me to include some of his father's jazz-related Family Circus cartoons in my books;

And especially my wife Carol, the most important person in my life, who was and is such a vital part in bringing this project to fruition.

Lew Shaw

DEDICATION: One of life's joys for **Richard Simkins**, a fellow Westminster Village resident, was playing his tenor saxophone in various bands. Unhappily, the sax now collects dust in his apartment closet as age and health issues have limited his ability to make music. But his love for good music has in no way diminished, and he has found that the best therapy for him at this stage of his life has been the hours he and I have shared listening to great jazz with an uplifting beat. As Richard has said on numerous occasions, "Music makes my life work."

DOWNBEAT

Lew Shaw cut his teeth as a jazz writer interviewing the likes of Armstrong, Ellington, Basie and Kenton while promoting a summer-long jazz and folk series held at the Berkshire Music Barn in Lenox, Massachusetts. For more than 30 years, he has been a staff writer and columnist for a succession of monthly newspapers that cover Traditional Jazz and Swing.

Lew Shaw interviewing Count Basie at the Berkshire Music Barn

Following his relocation to Arizona in 1984, he cofounded a jazz society that grew to 1,000 members under his leadership along with an annual festival; served as national president of the American Federation of Jazz Societies for three years; and is a past member of the Arizona Musicfest's jazz committee and current member of the Jazz Journalists Association.

After a lifetime as a reportorial writer, his first venture as a book author was his 2013 book, **JAZZ BEAT, Notes on Classic Jazz**, a collection of 47 profiles of musicians and jazz advocates.

AD LIBITUM

("performers decide how to play")

HOWARD ALDEN
Master of the Guitar

Published March 2017

A bibliography of **Howard Alden's** career provides some interesting benchmarks that delineate the impressive accomplishments of a musician who has been called "the most impressive and creative member of a new generation of jazz guitarists." To illustrate:

In 1990, *Jazz Times* designated him the "Best Emerging Guitar Talent."

Downbeat cited him four times as a "Talent Deserving of Wider Recognition" as well as including him on their list of Top Guitarists.

The American Guitar Museum named him "Guitar Player of the Year" in 2003.

He was chosen as the music director and guitarist for an all-star lineup selected to commemorate the 50th anniversary of the fabled Newport Jazz Festival that went on a tour of 50 U.S. cities in 2004.

Among his many accolades, one writer extolled: "His playing is classic, yet full of invention; distinctive, yet inspired by the work of the giants of jazz who were his tutors."

Growing up in Newport, California, Howard began playing the tenor banjo at the age of 10. He had lessons with a retired banjo player who taught him to read and introduced him to many of the vintage tunes commonly associated with the banjo. His first professional gigs were working pizza parlors in Southern California. "As a 12-year-old, I was considered a curiosity," he recalled.

He soon gravitated to a 4-string guitar, and after hearing recordings by Barney Kessel, Charlie Christian and Django Reinhardt, got a 6-string guitar, which he taught himself to play. In his late teens, he came under the tutelage of studio musician Howard Roberts and attended classes at the Guitar Institute of Technology in Hollywood.

Howard Alden made his first trip to the East Coast in the summer of 1979 to play in a trio led by Red Norvo at Resorts International in Atlantic City and continued to play with the legendary vibraphonist frequently for several years. He moved to New York City in 1982, and his skills both as a soloist and accompanist were soon recognized by such established musicians as Joe Bushkin, Woody Herman, Dick Hyman, Ruby Braff and Joe Williams, resulting in a busy schedule of appearances and recordings.

In 1987, he ran into some health issues that sapped his energy and cause him to lose consciousness temporarily ("black out") on occasion. The condition did not affect his motor skills, and he actually felt best when he was playing music. Over a matter of several years, he received numerous diagnoses, underwent surgeries and finally found specialists and a nutritionist at Emory University in Atlanta, Georgia, who identified his malady as Sarcoidosis, which is defined as "the growth of tiny collections of inflammatory cells in different parts of the body, resulting from the body's immune system responding to an unknown substance, most likely something inhaled from the air." There is no known cure, but in Howard's case, can be treated, and happily, he has been off medications for the past 10 years.

He signed with the Concord Jazz record label in 1988, an association which led to Alden recording with one of his all-time heroes, 7-string guitar master George Van Eps, on the album *Thirteen Strings* and three follow-up albums. Inspired by Van Eps, and recognizing that the 7-string imparts a greater range and harmonic richness, Howard has been playing the 7-string guitar since 1992.

"I'd been listening to George's records for many years and knew about the 7-string," he explained, "but I was never really motivated to start playing one because I was perfectly comfortable on the 6-string. It wasn't until I spent a few days in the studio with George and seeing how he handled the instrument was when it all suddenly clicked in for me. Bucky Pizzarelli was another who encouraged me to take up the 7-string guitar."

"An additional thing that drew me to the 7-string was when I would hear tunes by some of the great piano players that I wanted to play on the guitar, but needed a little extra range. One of my favorites was Bill Evans who often played in clusters of four or five notes in one octave, which is impossible when you're playing a 6-string guitar."

"Learning to play the guitar effectively is like learning a language. It's similar to opening a grammar book and memorizing every single rule of conjunctions and where the verb and adjective go. So it is with the guitar where you learn how to speak in phrases and how to utilize that approach correctly and to your advantage."

His advice to novice guitarists: "Young people need to build a repertoire of songs so that what they are playing isn't just technical ideas. Then they should commit that repertoire to memory to make it part of their musical language. If you have to look at a fakebook, you don't really know the tune. It's important to be more than an entertainer. I love to play what I call 'sincere music' that gets a response from the audience. Do your homework, and be prepared when that big opportunity comes along."

Howard was introduced to choro music when the late clarinetist Kenny Davern gave him a tape (that he had received from guitarist Charlie Byrd) by Jacob do Bandolin, the Brazilian composer and mandolin master who launched a choro revival in the 1940s. Choro music is referred to as "the New Orleans jazz of Brazil" and is described as "fast, happy rhythm full of syncopation and counterpoint."

"I fell in love with that cassette and didn't even know there was a genre called choro," Howard said. "It's such infectious music and has so many parallels with early jazz, ragtime and bebop." He subsequently discovered a small choro scene in New York City and enthusiastically joined some Brazilian musicians and fellow converts like clarinetist Anat Cohen (who has recorded several choro-inspired albums) in performing the music. He has since made six trips to Brazil to indulge in his expanding repertoire and exposure to this South American jazz hybrid.

Howard took his talents to the silver screen when he was asked to work with actor Sean Penn in his role as a tormented musician who describes himself as "the second greatest guitarist in the world" (obviously surpassed by the real guitar legend, Django Reinhardt) in Woody Allen's 1999 film, *Sweet and Lowdown*.

As Howard tells the story, "I got a call from Dick Hyman, with whom I have worked since 1983 and who does the music for most of Woody's films, asking if I could play like Django Reinhardt. I responded jokingly, 'Of course, Dick, doesn't everybody.' I was then asked to coach Sean on how to play the guitar. At first, I thought that would be a two or three day assignment, but it turned out to be five months of coaching."

"Sean had never touched a guitar before, so I helped him select the instruments for the movie. He was very serious and dedicated to learning what he had to do to play the part. I think he did an amazing job. When they would shoot a scene where Sean was playing the guitar, I would sit off camera and play the tune so Sean could see where my fingers were going."

"Dick Hyman wanted the combo in the film be a Hot Club of France with a violin. I mentioned that this was America in the 1930s, and the violin wasn't all that popular then. I suggested they have a clarinet and drummer, and they went with that idea. We picked Bucky Pizzarelli for the rhythm guitar on the soundtrack. It was a great experience to see a film made from the ground up and to be on the set every day."

After living in New York City for 33 years, Howard now resides in Arizona with his wife Diane. He's not resting on his laurels and continues to seek out new opportunities and experiences. If there is such a thing as a complete jazz guitarist, then Howard Alden is it.

JOEY ALEXANDER
Jazz's Newest Sensation

Published 2016

You've heard about this phenom of the keyboard from Indonesia. You've read the lavish praise served up by the pundits of the jazz community and media. And now you see this 13-year-old prodigy saunter onto the stage, clasp his hands and bow politely to the audience. He seats himself at the piano, and the magic begins. His virtuosity and musical sophistication are almost mind-boggling.

In just three years, **Joey Alexander** has become the hottest ticket on the jazz circuit. Wynton Marsalis, artistic director of Jazz at Lincoln Center, refers to Joey as "my hero," saying, "Joey Alexander is not someone or something you can even explain. We've never had anyone like him in this music, not with that harmonic maturity. I wasn't anywhere near his sophistication at his age, nor has anyone I know ever been. I love everything about his playing – his rhythm, his confidence, his understanding of the music."

For one so young, but who plays like a veteran, just consider:

▶ He is the youngest performer ever to be nominated for a Grammy music award;

▶ He's played at the White House, Lincoln Center, NYC Town Hall, and the youngest person to ever take the stage at the Newport Jazz Festival;

▶ His debut album, *My Favorite Things,* hit #1 on *Billboard's* Jazz Albums chart;

▶ CBS *60 Minutes* ran a 13-minute profile on Joey, and he jammed with NBC *Nightly News* anchor Lester Holt when he appeared on the *Today* show;

▶ *TIME* Magazine ran a feature that referred to him as a "Next Generation Leader" and "Master of the Keys."

According to an edited version of his Wikipedia bio, "Josiah Alexander Sila was born in the city of Denpasar in Bali, Indonesia to parents Denny Sila and Farah Leonora Urbach, who ran an adventure tourism business. His father was an amateur musician, and both parents were jazz fans, particularly the works of Louis Armstrong."

"Joey learned about jazz by listening to classic albums his father gave him. By age 6, he had taught himself to play the piano using a miniature electric keyboard and learning to play by ear compositions such as Monk's *Well, You Needn't* and other songs from his father's jazz collection. Joey said learning the instrument came naturally for him and considers his ability 'a gift from God.' Alexander considers Monk, John Coltrane, Harry Connick, Jr., Bill Evans and Herbie Hancock among his main musical influences and also admires Clifford Brown, Miles Davis, Wynton Marsalis, Horace Silver and McCoy Tyner."

"Due to the unavailability of formal jazz training where he grew up, Alexander began playing in jam sessions with experienced musicians in Bali and Jakarta, where his family moved after disbanding their tourism business so their son could be near Indonesia's top jazz musicians. Alexander played for Herbie Hancock at age 8 when the pianist was visiting Jakarta as a UNESCO goodwill ambassador.

14

Hancock told Alexander he believed in him, and Joey later described that as 'the day I decided to dedicate my childhood to jazz.' At age 9, he won the Grand Prix at the 2013 Master-Jam Fest, an all-ages jazz competition in Odessa, Ukraine, which included 43 musicians from 17 nations. Joey and his family moved to New York City in 2014."

Alexander's debut album, *My Favorite Things*, was released in May of 2015 when he was 11. He arranged all the songs in the album, which included renditions of *Round Midnight*, Coltrane's *Giant Steps* and Billy Strayhorn's *Lush Life*, plus an original composition called *Ma Blues*. Producer George Wein, who is normally reluctant to sign child prodigies, made an exception with Joey and booked him for the 2015 Newport Jazz Festival, where he received standing ovations for his performance. Jazz at Lincoln Center has expressed interest in incorporating him into its educational outreach efforts, hoping to encourage young people to listen to jazz music.

Joey clearly loves and respects his art form. "Jazz is hard work," he says, "and you really have to work at it, but you also should have fun performing." A devout Christian who is homeschooled, his daily routine involves alternating between bible study and three hours of practice on the piano. He considers himself a regular teenager. "I watch movies and play sports – a little tennis, swimming, like a normal kid." Through it all, Joey has remained humble, focused on developing as a player and pursuing his growing interest in composing. He is not comfortable with the constant reference to being a genius or prodigy, saying "I just want people to dig my music."

PAOLO ALDERIGHI
Spreading Joy for Jazz

Published October 2016

When asked for his first impression on meeting Stephanie Trick in 2008 at a festival in Switzerland, **Paolo Alderighi** responded without hesitation, "I was totally blown away. Here was this attractive young girl who played stride piano and liked Fats Waller. What more could you want."

So what was Stephanie's reaction? "The organizers at these festivals give you a program that lists with whom you're going to play. Since I was new at the time, I didn't know anyone. It turns out I was teamed with Paolo, and he was just the nicest person. He knew I was scared, but he was always there for me that weekend. And I loved the way he played. He has a unique approach that's a mix of all sorts of influences. The organizers at Boswil now take credit for having introduced us. I think they *wanted* to get us together."

Stephanie and Paolo with retired Supreme Court Justice Sandra Day O'Connor at a benefit for the Arizona State University School of Law

Paolo's father is an amateur jazz musician who still enjoys playing the double bass, banjo or harmonica, and Paolo has an older brother who plays the clarinet. So he grew up listening to a lot of classic jazz. At 16, he joined the Chicago-style Milano Jazz Gang. In 2000, he received his degree in music and piano from the G. Verdi Conservatory of Milan and then completed a five-year graduate program in economics for the arts, culture and media at Bocconi University, which is also located in his hometown of Milan, Italy.

In 2004, he won a prize as the best young musician at the Breda Festival in The Netherlands, which led to the first of five appearances at the Kobe Jazz Festival. It was at this point that it became obvious that Paolo's future career would be as a professional jazz pianist. *Musica Jazz* magazine substantiated that decision, ranking him second in the "Best New Talent" category and first in "Brand New Jazz Acts" by popular vote for the 2007 Italian jazz awards.

He was the recipient of a National Prize for the Arts in the jazz category by the Italian Ministry of University and Research. Paolo and Stephanie have been performing together for the past five years and have been married since 2013. They maintain an apartment in Milan and one in Stephanie's hometown of St. Louis, where her mother still lives. They admit the travel is intense, spending half of their time in the United States, and half in Europe, a schedule that involves six or seven trans-Atlantic trips in the course of a year.

A typical itinerary would find them performing in Switzerland, Germany, France and Sweden, followed by a week-long jazz cruise up the East Coast from New York City to Nova Scotia. Then off to the

Sun Valley Jazz & Music Festival in Idaho, and back across the Atlantic to Switzerland and England before returning to the United States for the West Coast Ragtime and San Diego Thanksgiving Festivals. Wrap up the year with a 10-day jazz cruise departing from Miami, Florida for various ports in the Caribbean, and then heading for Asia for the International Music Festival in Thailand. *Peripatetic* has to be the operative word for this itinerate couple.

Eighty-five percent of their performances are currently joint appearances. "You get used to being constantly on the move," Paolo acknowledges, "but the important thing is that Stephanie and I are together. We don't have a particular routine, and every day is different. We practice as much as we can and are always working on new arrangements. During the months of February and May, I teach a History of Music course at Bocconi University."

Paolo's first trip to the United States was in 2011 to perform at the Arbors Records Invitational Jazz Party in Clearwater Beach, Florida. He retains his Italian citizenship, but is considered a permanent resident of the United States as a Green Card holder. In what little spare time he has, he enjoys reading, especially about the history of America and its music.

A highlight for Stephanie and Paolo was the opportunity to play for the Prince of Wales and Duchess of Cornwall (who are known as the Duke and Duchess of Rothesay in Scotland) at the Edinburgh Jazz & Blues Festival in 2014.

While each has their own distinctive style, they have definitely found a basis for compatibility in the five years they have been together, whether it's on one piano or two. Stephanie focuses on James P. Johnson, Fats Waller and Albert Ammons, while Paolo leans more toward Erroll Garner, Earl "Fatha" Hines and Teddy Wilson. The title of their first CD together in 2014 says it best: *Two for One,* along with demonstrating their great enthusiasm and passion for classic jazz.

As Dick Hyman has stated, "I love to hear Stephanie Trick and Paolo Alderighi together. They are an inspiration. Such sympatico! Such back-and-forth! Individually they are marvelous musicians - we've known that, but together they play 4-handed stride as it's never been done. Brava, bravo!"

"The alphabet on pianos only goes up to 'G,' then starts over."

HARRY ALLEN
Tops on the Tenor Sax

Published April 2014

Harry Allen has been identified as one of the finest proponents of the swing tenor saxophone alive today, a traditionalist in the manner of Scott Hamilton, who favors the Great American Songbook and time-tested standards. One critic called him "the Frank Sinatra of the tenor saxophone, a master interpreter of standards." He cites Ben Webster, Stan Getz, Coleman Hawkins and Lester Young as having influenced his style.

Stan Getz was once asked his idea of the perfect saxophone soloist. His answer was "My technique, Al Cohn's ideas and Zoot Sims' time." The fulfillment of that ideal may well be embodied in 47-year-old Harry Allen. A review of his press clippings makes note that he is consistently reliable and endlessly adaptable, constantly in demand, prolific, versatile, inventive, thoughtful and resourceful, smooth and bold, and especially appreciated by the musicians with whom he works - easygoing, affable and tireless. That's a tough reputation to live up to, but Harry takes it all in stride.

He loves and plays all sorts of jazz from Traditional to Modern and describes his sound as "big, round and warm with a lot of air in it – a '40s sound." He goes on to say, "The sound is the most important thing." Pianist Rossano Sportiello, who frequently plays in Harry's quartet, comments, "I've yet to find a tune that Harry didn't know. He's got incredible facility playing at any tempo, in any key, and within different styles, always with great taste and an excellent quality of sound and powerful swing. His time and pitch are perfect, and he can improvise like a volcano, phrase after phrase, and you'll never hear him playing patterns or repeated licks."

What drives him? "I just like to play and am perfectly content to play a song that I may not especially like." For many of his albums, he leaves repertoire decisions up to the label head. He sees his job as simply to make the best of what is handed to him. "On one of my earlier tours, I learned an important lesson from an older musician who told me that I should play every song as if it was my all-time favorite." The late Jake Hanna once told him, "It's all about the music and surviving."

He doesn't play a lot of notes when a few will do. He's a purist at heart and admits to being a bit of a perfectionist. "The important thing is not to lose the intent of the song. I like to check the sheet music and get an idea of what the composer had in mind. I may change a few things, but I try not to lose sight of the overall picture."

Harry was born in Washington, DC and spent his early years in Los Angeles. His father was an engineer by trade and a part-time drummer who had played with Arvell Shaw, Paul Gonsales and the songwriter Johnny Burke. (Appropriately, Harry has done a CD of tunes from the Burke-Jimmy Van Heusen songbook entitled *Conversations*.) The accordion was the first musical instrument for Harry and his sister, with Dad on the drums for family jam sessions. The elder Allen had an extensive record collection, and Harry remembers, "What I heard was compelling music, and it drew me in right away."

Harry says he knew early on that he wanted to play the saxophone and to be a professional musician. He initially took up the clarinet when he was given one by a friend of his father. At the age of 12, he picked up the tenor sax, saying, "I always had the tenor sound in my head."

The family moved back to the East Coast where Harry graduated from Burrillville High School in Rhode Island. It wasn't long before he was recognized for his exceptional talent and uncanny ability to play such tunes as *Body and Soul* in the style of legendary tenor players Coleman Hawkins, Ben Webster, Flip Phillips and Sam Donahue. In 1983-84 at age of 17, he was a member of the McDonald's All-American High School Band.

When it came time for college, he decided he didn't want to attend a major music school and enrolled at Rutgers University in New Jersey where he majored in music and graduated in 1988. He soon was playing with the Pizzarellis, Major Holley and Oliver Jackson. One time Bucky Pizzarelli hired Harry as a sub for Stan Getz. During the set, he recalls that Dizzy Gillespie walked in, and Harry said he was so scared that he was shaking like a leaf in the presence of the great trumpeter.. "I learned my craft sitting in with bands," he states.

He had a long-standing working relationship with Scott Hamilton (whom Harry considers a mentor). John Pizzarelli introduced him to a Japanese record producer, and Harry began recording exclusively for the Japanese market. John once brought Harry to California to do a tenor sax overdub at a recording session. He did it on the first and only take, to which composer-arranger Johnny Mandel who was present quipped, "Does this guy ever make a mistake?"

Harry is featured on many of John Pizzarelli's recordings, including the soundtrack and an on-screen cameo appearance in the feature film, *The Out of Towners* staring Goldie Hawn and Steve Martin. He also did a series of commercials for ESPN featuring the late Robert Goulet.

In his book, *World on a String: A Musical Memoir,* John Pizzarelli tells of an early encounter Harry had with the great Benny Goodman. Goodman had been hired to play at a wedding and asked the elder Pizzarelli to line up the musicians. Bucky thought Harry's sound would be great for Benny and invited the young tenor whiz to the rehearsal.

According to John, in those days it took Harry a good 10 minutes to get ready to play. "Soak the reeds, wipe down the sax, wash, rinse, repeat . . .until you finally wanted to hit him in the back and shout, 'Get on with it!'"

Harry sat by patiently while the band rehearsed for 40 minutes. After a short break, the band kicked off with *Avalon*. Here John picks up the story: "While Benny was blowing, he pointed his clarinet as a signal for Harry to take out his sax. It was the only time I have ever seen Harry unpack his sax, skip the preliminaries, and be ready to play in seconds flat. Benny had that power."

23

The Harry Allen Quartet includes Joe Cohn on guitar, Joel Forbes on bass and Chuck Riggs or Kevin Kanner on drums, with Rossano Sportiello on piano when the group goes without a guitar. The quartet has played all the major clubs from Feinstein's (before it closed) and Birdland in New York City to Yoshi's in San Francisco and has received several awards as the top jazz combo.

Harry has made over 40 recordings under his own name in the Japanese market alone and is a staple with Arbor Records. He is on the road 30 weeks a year, including three or four European tours. "The constant flying is tiring," he says, "but I'm not tired of playing." He has lived in the Big Apple for the past 30 years and stays in shape playing tennis.

Rebecca Kilgore sums to up best, saying "It's a real joy to work with Harry. So many jazz musicians are difficult or have huge egos. Harry just flies in the face of that stereotype. He is so calm and doesn't get ruffled. Plus he may be just about the best musician that I know."

THE FAMILY CIRCUS.   By Bil Keane

"All these little golf clubs are called 'notes.'"

JOHN ALLRED
Carrying on the Family Legacy

Published March 2016

From great-grandmother to grandfather to father to son. That's the musical legacy of the Allred family.

John Allred's great-grandmother was born near New Orleans in Franklin, Louisiana. His grandfather John was a jazz pianist and banjoist who played on the steamboats of the famed Streckfus Line that plied the Mississippi and Ohio rivers. Father Bill is a highly-regarded trombonist - still active - who has had a 45-year career at Disney World and venues in Florida and heading his own band.

John knew at an early age that he wanted to carry on the family jazz legacy. Born in Rock Island, Illinois and growing up in a musical environment, he soon developed a deep appreciation for jazz. "My Dad collected instruments, and he was always listening to his father's early jazz records," John recalled. "He had a huge respect for traditional jazz, which made a big impression on me."

The family moved to Florida in 1971 when Bill was one of the first musicians hired at Disney World. Rehearsals were held at the Allred home after which the musicians would sit around, drink beer and tell stories. John learned the vocabulary of jazz by listening and was surprised at the number of tunes he knew.

John's first opportunity to go on stage was at Rosie O'Grady's Goodtime Emporium on Church Street in Orlando when he was dressed in the same attire as the band members. At the age of 13, John played his first festival on trombone with his father: the Bix in Davenport, Iowa. Bill advised his son, "Stand next to me and watch what I do." John admits to being awestruck, but came away with a great feeling for having played the entire festival.

John with his Dad Bill on the bandstand

Upon graduation from high school, John relocated to Southern California to start playing professionally with The Jazz Minors, a six-piece Dixieland jazz band at Disneyland in Anaheim. Still in his teens, John was soon caught up in the Los Angeles music scene that included being a member of Dave Wells Trombone City and recording with the Los Angeles Jazz Workshop. In addition to his interest in early jazz, he ventured into other musical styles. This versatility allowed him many opportunities to perform with big bands and studio orchestras.

Now married, it was back to Florida in 1986 where John became active in the jazz and studio scenes that involved Disney World, Broadway shows, even the circus. He toured for a time with Harry Connick Jr's big band. For the major motion picture, *My Girl*, he coached actor Dan Ackroyd to appear as if he were playing the tuba, and John recorded the tuba parts for the sound track.

In 1987, John accepted an offer to join Woody Herman and the Young Thundering Herd as lead trombonist and featured soloist. During his three years with Woody's band, John played in hundreds of clubs, concert halls and colleges across the nation, including Carnegie Hall and the Kennedy Center, while performing with the likes of Rosemary Clooney, Tony Bennett, Clark Terry, Buddy DeFranco, Terry Gibbs and Stan Getz.

"It was another great experience," John recalled. "Everything we did was focused on the music. You had to be perfect in what you were doing, and everybody played their best."

Returning to Orlando, John began working more with his father in Bill Allred's Classic Jazz Band. He led a euphonium band, worked at Rosie O'Grady's and the MGM Studios,, and performed in many production shows for headliners such as: Ray Charles, Natalie Cole, Paul Anka, Wayne Newton, Don Rickles, Joan Rivers, Regis Philbin and Kathy Lee, the Moody Blues, The Temptations and The Four Tops.

John's first jazz party was at Indianapolis in 1988 where he met Jake Hanna, Ralph Sutton, Bob Haggart and Yank Lawson who took an interest in furthering the young trombonist's career. It was about this time that John expanded his horizon when he was invited to play at festivals in Europe. In 1990, John accepted a spot with the famed Matteson-Phillips Tuba-Jazz Consort, a unique ensemble that featured John on euphonium alongside jazz great Rich Matteson and famous tubist Harvey Phillips.

John released his first trombone solo recording, *In the Beginning,* with Arbors Records in 1993. The year 1999 saw John Allred move to New York City where he has performed with groups such as Toshiko Akiyoshi's Big Band, the Woody Herman Orchestra under the direction of Frank Tiberi, the Carnegie Hall Jazz Band, as well as productions for Dick Hyman, and George Wein for the JVC Jazz Festival.

When not off to a festival or jazz party these days, John can be found playing in a Broadway show orchestra, which he views as a regular job with salary and health benefits. Saying "one has to be a good reader," his list of credits includes *Pajama Game, How to Succeed in Business, Cinderella, Bullets over Broadway* and *Finding Neverland.*

Looking at the past and future, he says "I've enjoyed traveling the world, but at the age of 53, I also enjoy being able to stay home for extended periods. I hope to do more writing, and I especially like playing in small groups. I enjoy every style of jazz and always strive to do my best. I especially want to gain the respect of the musicians I respect. I have no great desire to be famous. I just want to play music that people enjoy and that I enjoy as well."

JIM ARMSTRONG
Forever Young

Published November 2014

Jim Armstrong must have discovered the Fountain of Youth because he is still playing rugby at the age of 75.

Rugby is not a game for 90-pound weaklings or the faint-of-heart. It is a contact sport originated in England in the early 1800s and is the British grammar schools' game of choice. Jim has participated in the sport since the seventh grade. He describes it to his American friends as "football without pads and helmets, without blocking or forward passing, and without stopping every eight seconds to have a meeting to decide what to do next."

In the 1980s, he discovered Over-40 rugby being played by several teams in Vancouver and Victoria. The players wear outfits that are color-coded by age: the 40-year-olds are in white shorts, the 50's, black; 60's, red; and 70's, yellow. The rules prohibit tackling the yellow-clad 70-year-olds, but Jim will usually abstain from wearing his yellow shorts unless someone is doing so on the opposing team, "I don't see the point of playing the game without full contact," he contends.

He acknowledges the danger of injury and admits he's had a broken nose twice as well as a broken wrist, which ironically was caused by one of his teammates. He feels he has been able to avoid serious injury because of the position he plays, describing it as the American football equivalent of running back/wide receiver. "I can stay away from those large brutish fellows who do all the hard work in the scrum."

"I can still run faster than some of the guys on our team who are 10 to 20 years younger who consider me an inspiration of sorts," he modestly admits. His team – the Semiahmoo Old Boys (a.k.a. SOBs) –

won a tournament in New Orleans, and Jim was named his team's MVP.

Jazz fans identify Jim with his past association with the Phoenix Jazzers and CanUS and currently with Grand Dominion. It was the 34th Company of the Boys Brigade, a variation of the scouting movement, that got him into music. His friends were in the brass band sponsored by the local Presbyterian church in Belfast, and he joined so as to be with them. His first instrument was an E-flat alto horn, which he calls the most boring instrument in the world. "You play all the inner parts and have nothing important to do. I discovered I knew all the notes to play without having to read them. I could hear the changes, but I didn't know anything about chords and such."

He soon graduated to a euphonium, or baritone horn, but realized that instrument is not found in a jazz band. The Trad fad was then in full swing in Britain, and Chris Barber, Ken Colyer and Acker Bilk were his favorites. He switched to trombone, and a friend gave him some basic instructions on how to play the instrument. He acknowledges to this day he doesn't read music very well, and he commits tunes to memory listening to records.

While in teacher's college in Ireland, he and a friend formed a band, the Embankment Six, that soon developed a following. That led to a stint with a show band that could play any type of music, which greatly expanded Jim's ability to play in different keys and a wide range of styles. Feeling teaching opportunities were limiting in Northern Ireland., he emigrated to Canada in 1966, ending up in rural Alberta, which he describes as akin to living in Wyoming with "no jazz for two years." He moved to Vancouver in 1968 and played casuals with the Old Style Jazz Band.

Mike Cox worked in the same school district, and it was through him that Jim joined the Phoenix Jazzers in 1979. "Mike called and said he had lost his trumpet and trombone players and would I be interested in joining the band,' Jim recalled. "I figured if I played trombone I'd be doing the same thing I'd been doing for years. So I thought about taking up the trumpet. The trumpet basically plays the melody, and I knew a lot of tunes. I'd played the euphonium in high school, and the fingering is the same. I just needed to get used to the smaller mouthpiece. So I borrowed a trumpet from a student at the school where I was teaching and became a trumpeter."

"People often asked me which instrument I prefer. I think I am much better on trombone. When I'm praised for my ability on both instruments, I remember a quotation attributed to Winston Churchill, who when referring to a political rival, said, 'A modest little gentleman with much to be modest about'."

Originally from Wales, Mike Cox was steeped in the music of the New Orleans revivalist musicians like George Lewis, Bunk Johnson, Baby Dodds and Kid Ory. So in 1982, he recruited a group of his expatriated friends from both sides of the U.S.-Canada border to form Grand Dominion, a band that over the years has embodied all the rough-and-ready, hard-driving ensemble characteristics of the revivalist bands. "We just clicked," Jim said, and the band became a regular at the Hot Jazz Club of Vancouver and on the festival circuit.

"Three of us came from the Jazzers: Mike on banjo, Gerry Green on clarinet, and me on trombone. From Seattle came Bob Jackson, trumpet, and Mike Duffy, bass, of the Excelsior JB; Bob Pelland, piano, of Rainier JB; and Steve Joseph, drums, of Uptown Lowdown." As Grand Dominion's star rose, bookings for the Jazzers declined. Mike Cox retired to a stone cottage in Cornwall England, and Pelland took over leadership of Grand Dominion as did Jim with the Jazzers, who continued to play until 2002.

In 1990, Jim took a leave from his Vancouver teaching job and went to check out Victoria as a possibility for later retirement. While there, Toni Blodgett approached him about singing in a Christmas carol quartet since he had been singing in the Vancouver Bach Choir. The plan was to perform in local hotels and restaurants during the holiday season, but by the time the group was ready, all the possible openings has been booked.

Toni thought, "Hey, if we can sing carols, we can sing anything – Boswell Sisters, Mills Brothers and all those great tunes from the Hot

20s and Swinging 30s." Such was the beginning of CanUs, with Toni on piano, Jim on trumpet and trombone, Joey Smith on bass, and Don Leppard, the only non-singer, on drums. CanUs became a popular festival draw and has been playing Sundays at Hermann's Jazz Club in Victoria for the past 24 years. Jim left the band when he retired from teaching in 1998 and now resides with his wife Vicki in White Rock, B.C.

Asked what occupies his time in retirement, he replies, "*Nothing* . . . and I'm very good at it." He still practices an hour nearly every day. He follows baseball and says if there is a Life Hereafter, he'd like to come back as the third baseman for the New York Yankees (which relates back to when he listened to Yankee games on Armed Forces radio broadcasts as a youth). As he reflects on his long and busy career, he ruminates, "I have always realized my limitations, albeit self-imposed, and never felt inclined to go to the lengths to be become 'great.' Rather I like to think that I am well-prepared for any given gig with any given band. I will always play my part and not let anyone down."

As he continued his self-analysis, he acknowledged to being painfully shy. "I know this will come as a surprise to many fans, but I am not good at mixing with people. I may put on a good act while on-stage, but off-stage, I let others carry the conversation while I prefer to be a good listener."

Grand Dominion's Bob Pelland first met Jim in 1977 and offered some insights on the band's popular trombonist-vocalist. "Because of his lifelong participation in rugby, Jim brings an absolute team attitude towards the band. He never slacks off and delivers 100% even when he's not feeling his best. He has near-perfect pitch and a keen sense of harmony. Jim may joke, 'Show me the green, and I'll make the scene,' but it goes way beyond that. His encyclopedic memory keeps him right on top of the hundreds of vocals he performs so well. He's also adept at making up a word or two if there's a slip."

Bob adds, "For years, Jim has been the 'trivia master' of the band with answers to the most ridiculous questions. He often makes up little tests of knowledge, usually asking us Americans bits of our history that we should know. It's something that dates back to his youthful fascination with all things having to do with the United States when, for example, he could name all the states and their capitals."

Bob concludes, "Jim loves a nice pint of ale and good companions at the pub which we all seem to find on our many band trips. It's been a superb trip to know and work with this fine musician for these many years."

"Don't tackle anybody bigger than you are!"

EVAN ARNTZEN
5th Generation Going Strong

Published April 2018

Four generations of **Evan Arntzen's** family have been merry music makers covering more than 100 years. Evan's great-grandfather came to America from Norway in 1908 and played the banjo and sang. It was grandfather Lloyd, still going strong at age 90, who had the greatest influence on Evan and his younger brother, Arnt. Both of their parents have had successful careers as professional musicians.

During the heydays of Dixieland festivals, clarinetist-soprano saxophonist Lloyd Arntzen was well known as the leader of the New Orleans North Traditional Jazz Band, Broadway Swells and Dixieland Express as well as a member of the Sweet Papa Lowdown band. Every Wednesday, he would pick up his grandsons from school and take them to his home where he would give them lessons on their instruments as well as in woodworking.

In 2006, Gwendoline Records issued a live CD titled *3 Generations on Jazz* recorded live at Vancouver's Cellar Jazz Café that included Lloyd, his two sons and two grandsons. Another family project was *Blackstick*, released in 2013 and recorded in Lloyd's basement over three days.

Evan's father Tom has been a pianist, singer and bandleader in Vancouver for the past 30 years. He plays piano, organ and accordion and as he puts it, specializes in handclaps. His forte is his renditions of contemporary favorites and tunes from the Great American Songbook along with some mellow crooning a la Frank Sinatra.

Evan follows the example of his grandfather Lloyd

As the distaff side, Evan's vocalizing mother Georgina is a member of the Hot Mammas Trio and once toured North America in a converted bus. She has made numerous TV appearances, teaches music and cuts a mean Klondike Kate.

Younger brother Arnt plays acoustic guitar, banjo and sings, is a songwriter and leads his own band, A Pluckin' Good Time. He has produced his own album of original material, called *Banjo Hymn*. He and Evan collaborate in leading several bands, namely The Brothers Arntzen, the Arntzen Rhythm Review and Three Generations of Jazz.

Having been born into this musical family in Vancouver, British Columbia, Evan got an early start when he learned about traditional jazz from grandfather Lloyd at the age of 7. He had a band as a youth, played in his high school concert band, and says he has always had a positive view of jazz because it is something he enjoys. In fact, he even considers it a point of pride. He obtained a B.A. in Saxophone Performance from Capilano University in Vancouver, although he feels that jazz education is missing a lot, but acknowledges he did learn valuable lessons during his jazz studies experience.

Evan spent a year with the Jim Cullum Jazz Band in San Antonio and was a featured soloist for the opening ceremonies of the Paralympic Games in 2010. He performed with Michael Bublé's orchestra in the 2012 and 2013 *Home for the Holidays* TV specials, as well as the Dinah Washington Tribute Concert with Jaclyn Guillou on CBC TV.

As he gained experience and recognition as a clarinetist, saxophonist and vocalist, Evan was the recipient of several awards, such as the Mayor of Vancouver's Arts Award as an Emerging Artist in Music (2010), the Kobe Award at the Breda Jazz Festival in the Netherlands (2010), and the Grand Prix de Jazz at the 2009 Montreal Jazz Festival (with the Amanda Tosoff Quartet).

Feeling that he had reached a certain level being based in Canada, he moved to New York City in 2014 and made connections with Vince Giordano' Nighhawks, Terry Waldo's Gotham City Band and Jon-Erik Kellso's EarRegulars. He has performed at some of New York's most prestigious venues such as Town Hall, Symphony Space, Dizzy's Club Coca-Cola, Birdland, Smalls and the Appel Room at Jazz at Lincoln Center.

 In 2015, he recorded with the Nighthawks on the soundtrack to the HBO film *Bessie*, a biographical film about Bessie Smith. He is also the co-leader of the Animule Dance, a quartet of young musicians possessing a unique interplay and frequently appears alongside 2017 Grammy-nominated vocalist Catherine Russell, daughter of legendary bandleader Luis Russell.

His travels have taken him throughout the United States and Canada. He has been a guest soloist at festivals in the Netherlands, France, Hungary and Japan. His long-time musical partnership with fellow Canadian, trumpeter-vocalist Bria Skonberg, continues to this day. As a member of Bria's quintet, Evans performed at the 2015 Newport Jazz Festival, the 2016 New Orleans Jazz & Heritage Festival, and recorded on her 2017 JUNO Award-winning Sony Records album, *Bria.*

While he plays many styles, Evan feels his roots are in traditional jazz. For all that he has accomplished in his 33 years, he modestly acknowledges "I feel I'm just getting started." In writing the liner notes for Evan's latest CD, – *Evan Arntzen Meets La Section Rythmique* that was recorded in France, the eminent retired *Downbeat* editor, Dan Morgenstern writes: "Evan has a distinctive style on both his chosen instruments, on which he offers appealing sounds, fluent command, and that often elusive thing called Swing."

EHUD ASHERIE
A Jazz Polymath

Published January 2019

Ehud Asherie has definitely taken a circuitous route to becoming a professional musician. The 39-year-old pianist was born in Israel, lived in Italy for six years before the family moved to the United States, and learned his trade as a teen-ager hanging out at a Greenwich Village jazz club where he was "old-schooled" by older musicians and where he made his professional debut when he was only a sophomore in high school.

A master of swing and stride, he is now known as a jazz pianist who integrates the venerable New York tradition into his inventive style. "It's an in-the moment thing where you take a lot of chances, are more melodically creative, and can present new rhythmic ideas," he declares.

One critic called him "a chameleon-like pianist" where one minute you may be hearing James P. Johnson or Fats Waller, followed by Monk or Bud Powell or a subtle Dick Hyman. Another wrote, "Asherie is no retrograde nostalgia peddler, but an adventurous, unrelenting, inventive young jazz polymath, playing everything from Louis Armstrong to Charlie Parker, and making it all his own."

Ehud is named for a character in the Old Testament of the Bible. His father, now retired, was in sales for the American President Lines, the world's largest container transportation and shipping company. Ehud describes his mother as "a traditional Jewish mother" who has always been involved in the arts and even today takes ballet lessons twice a week. Growing up, all five of the Asherie children played an instrument.

Taking up the piano at age 6 and largely self-taught, Ehud acknowledges that it was not one of his favorite things to do during his formative years. It wasn't until he discovered jazz listening to a Thelonious Monk CD, followed by his first visit to Smalls Jazz Club when he was 14 years old, that he found his true passion. "It was a live scene happening before me, and I was hooked," he remembers.

When it opened in 1993 in Greenwich Village in Lower Manhattan, Smalls was known as a hotbed for up-and-coming jazz talent, and the atmosphere was described as "young Bohemian and talkative." Music started at 10:30pm and lasted until 6am the following morning. Currently, the Club has a capacity of 60 and has curtailed the all-night sessions. The first of two or three set begins at 7:30pm.

It was at Smalls that Ehud learned the ropes, making the hour-long trek from the family home in Westchester County and often staying until the wee hours of the morning while getting a musical education from old timers like pianist Frank Hewitt and drummers Jimmy Lovelace and Frank Grant. Because the Club didn't have a liquor license at the time, he was able to stay for the late-night jam sessions. "My parents trusted me when they knew I was at Smalls, but when I went out with my friends, it was a different story," he recalls.

A year at the New College followed high school, but he found "I got more out of playing at clubs around town than I did from the academic experience. I have pretty much come up the old fashioned way: learning by playing. In a sense, I worked backwards in that I was initially influenced by the beboppers, but eventually came to appreciate the 100-plus years of jazz history and performance, and especially the contributions of piano greats like James P. Johnson and Fats Waller.

As he expanded his repertoire and developed his virtuosity and ear for clean, crisp lines, Ehud transitioned from Smalls to the Rainbow Room high atop Rockefeller Center where he had a 22-month engagement, working six-nights a week. From Lincoln Center to the Village Vanguard, he has toured clubs and festivals around the world and can be heard on the 2010 Grammy Award-winning soundtrack of HBO's *Boardwalk Empire*.

His early CDs were a mix of bop, swing and standards, with an occasional touch of stride. But the mainstay of his playing today is the music of the 1920s and '30s, which he explains is from a time when American songwriting had not yet calcified into the formulas we know today.

Beyond his dedication to jazz, he has also developed a passion for tradition Brazilian music. His appreciation and profound knowledge of the music, language and culture are the foundation for a project entitled Bina & Ehud, a duo formed in 2003, with Brazilian guitarist Bina Coquet. Most recently, he has been performing the works of Brazilian composer and pianist Ernesto Nazareth (1863-1934), who was noted for combining diverse influences into his music, often drawing on European and African themes as well as ragtime.

"Many Brazilian tunes are similar to those in the Great American Songbook. I'm always looking to find new outlets. Besides, when performing in New York, you're expected to know the bossa nova."

As he keeps busy as a soloist, leader of a trio or a sideman and traveling both in this country and internationally roughly 40 per cent of his time, he commented, "I want to be able to always play great tunes with great musicians and to have the ability to communicate with other people. Music is like a language. It always tells a story."

He likes to dig up old songs that are deserving to be heard, but are not well-known and cites as an example, *Flying Down to Rio,* a tune that was sung by Fred Astaire in a 1933 film. "These are songs that are cliché-free, free of harmonic patterns that allow so much freedom, and can be interpreted in so many different ways. There is not just one way to play a tune. They are a constant work in progress."

DAN BARRETT

Keeping a Legacy Alive

Published August 2014

When **Dan Barrett** meets strangers and tells them he is a professional musician, the inevitable question is: "With whom do you play?" Dan's standard answer is: "Many people," and that is an apt description of Dan's multi-faceted career that has covered the past four decades.

A native Californian, Dan was born in Pasadena and raised in nearby Costa Mesa. "It all began with some 78s my father often played," he said. "Artie Shaw's *Stardust* with that memorable solo by Jack Jenney; a recording by Lil Armstrong's band that included J.C. Higginbottom; and a Brunswick reissue of Red Nichols band featuring Jack Teagarden on *Indiana* and *Dinah*."

"Those were big influences on my trombone playing. The New Orleans style really grabbed me. I loved Kid Ory and Big Jim Robinson and later Miff Mole, Vic Dickenson, Tommy Dorsey, Dicky Wells, Lawrence Brown, Bill Harris and Bob Brookmeyer." "Critics often refer to how jazz 'developed' over the years, but I prefer the word 'changed.' Development implies improvement. The music didn't necessarily 'improve,' but it has certainly changed. We're the ones who just play music and try to make it swing. It's all part of the language of music."

"I sometimes refer to myself as a pre-bopper, because I love to hear Charlie Parker. I just don't speak the Parker dialect as well as the dialect from the Swing Era and before. I try to sing through my horn like Johnny Hodges, Jack Teagarden, Ben Webster and especially Louis Armstrong. It's an extension of my lifelong love affair with traditional jazz and the Great American Songbook."

Barrett began playing the trombone at the age of 11, and the cornet shortly thereafter. He formed his first band while in high school – the Back Bay Jazz Band – that included his future brother-in-law Bryan Shaw. While still in his teens, he had the opportunity to play with some of the great New Orleans musicians who had settled in Southern California: Barney Bigard, Nappy Lamare, Joe Darensbourg, Alton Purnell and Ed "Montudie" Garland.

Trombonist Al Jenkins, a long-overlooked hero of the West Coast jazz scene, had a strong influence on the developing talents of the teen-age Barrett. Recalling his first meeting with Jenkins, Dan said, "His ensemble playing was different than any I had heard up to that time. He literally had his own way of swinging. He found just the right notes to impart the fullest harmony and delivered them with that utterly relaxed, irresistible swing. I felt I was in the presence of greatness."

At age 17, he played *Ory's Creole Trombone* at the conclusion of Ory's funeral at Forest Lawn in January 1973, along with Teddy Buckner, Andy Blakeney and Alton Redd, all past members of Ory's band. In 1977 at the age of 22, he made the first of many trips to Europe to appear at the Breda Festival in Holland.

Dan and his wife Laura moved to New York City in 1983 where he toured with and wrote for the Widespread Depression Orchestra and was a frequent guest at Eddie Condon's, then managed by Ed Polcer. Dan played the valve trombone on the soundtrack of the 1984 movie, *The Cotton Club*, which led to more soundtrack credits and his first on-screen cameo in *Bullets Over Broadway*, a 1994 crime-comedy written and directed by Woody Allen, in which, to no surprise, Dan's role was as a trombonist.

He was a member of Benny Goodman's last orchestra (1985-86). He made a three-week tour of Europe with Woody Allen's' New Orleans Jazz Band in 1996, which later evolved into an award-winning documentary. His four appearances at Carnegie Hall included two Louis Armstrong tribute concerts with the New York Pops Orchestra.

His first original composition to be recorded was *The Minor Infraction*, a Basie-inspired swing number, recorded by the Dan Barrett Octet for Concord Records in 1987. He recorded a CD with famed cabaret singer Bobby Short that received a GRAMMY nomination. He composed and arranged the theme music for the American Playhouse production of *Rocket to the Moon* and the 2002 movie *The Sleepy Time Gal* starring Jacqueline Bisset.

The family returned to California in 1996 after living in New York City for 14 years and currently reside in Costa Mesa where son Andrew has a budding career as a freelance pianist with a swing band and at Disneyland's Ragtime Corner on Main Street. In 1998, Dan's songwriting abilities came to the attention of Canadian David Schacker, who was writing both the script and lyrics for a full-length animated feature, *The Jazz Bears*. Dan wrote five songs for the film, and he, Rebecca Kilgore and Eddie Erickson are the voices of three of the bear-characters. Unfortunately the film didn't make it out of production due to lack of financing.

He was the unofficial musical director for Arbors Records and has performed on some 40 CDs as both leader and sideman with such stalwarts as Rosemary Clooney, Doc Cheatham, Bob Haggart, Ruby Braff, Jay McShann, Buck Clayton and Howard Alden. More recently, he has been doing considerable arranging for small groups and big bands in the USA and Europe.

Dan is a popular draw at jazz parties and festivals around the country, usually in the company of his longtime cohorts, Becky Kilgore, "Fast Eddie" Erickson and bassist Joel Forbes where he's known to sit down at the piano for a few numbers on occasion. Dan is credited with "discovering" Rossano Sportiello at the 1998 Ascona, Switzerland Festival and underwriting the talented pianist's first CD. A number of other musicians have credited Barrett as contributing to their success.

John S. Wilson, the late-great *New York Times* jazz writer, called Dan "a melodist, a colorist who knows how to use a plunger mute with taste...a player Duke Ellington would have loved." Recognized in 1999 polls as the *Trombonist of the Year* and *Favorite Living Trombonist*, Dan has been listed in *Biographical Encyclopedia of Jazz* and *Guinness Who's Who of Jazz.*

Dan credits his parents and grandfather for instilling a love of reading, which now helps pass the time on his long transcontinental flights. He has a preference for the works of "hard-boiled" mystery writers like Dashiell Hammett and Raymond Chandler. When he's not on the road, he can be found at Disneyland playing trombone with Rusty Stiers' Jambalaya Jazz Band in the vicinity of New Orleans Square or cornet with Kenny Treseder's Royal Street Bachelors.

It's been a peripatetic life, which has become increasing difficult for a traveling musician with multiple instruments, but it's been a rewarding one for the affable Barrett, who is greatly respected and admired by his peers and jazz fans alike, and whose lifelong goal has been to keep a legacy alive. Just as he felt a sense of greatness on first hearing Al Jenkins, so has Dan Barrett achieved comparable stature in his chosen profession as a performer, arranger, composer, mentor and classic jazz advocate.

THE FAMILY CIRCUS. By Bil Keane

"I bet that's where they got the idea for paper clips."

DAVE BENNETT
Goodman to Jerry Lee Lewis

Published July 2015

According to his website, **Dave Bennett** doesn't fit the mold.

For starters, you don't find many jazz clarinet players who name Alice Cooper, Stevie Ray Vaughan and Chris Isaak among their influences (on a list that first-and-foremost, includes Benny Goodman along with Pete Fountain and Irving Fazola). Not many musicians in their early 30s are equally conversant with the music of Goodman (the "King of Swing") and Roy Orbison ("The Soul of Rock and Roll"). There may not be another clarinet virtuoso who occasionally breaks from his Swing Era repertoire to sing rockabilly hits while accompanying himself at the piano – where he plays a mean barrelhouse boogie-woogie.

Dave has been able to fuse serious jazz improvisation with a host of modern pop influences. He stays within the mainstream repertoire, and even covers several of the most famous hit records of the 1930s by Goodman as well as Woody Herman and Artie Shaw. But he updates these songs with intriguing twists and surprising new arrangements. In the process, he blazes his own path while still acknowledging his predecessors as he spotlights the jazz clarinet for a new generation.

"Since my early teens," says the Michigan-based clarinetist, "I've been influenced by many other genres besides jazz. My clarinet solo on a particular tune keeps the same basic outline, but it's different every time I play it. It may be based on chord progressions I hear on movie soundtracks, or I may steal licks from Alice Cooper or Stevie Ray Vaughan and other blues guitarists, just to achieve a certain sound or feeling. I think I'm finally finding my own voice, and I try to make each solo as dramatic as possible, so people wouldn't say I was just copying Benny."

Dave acknowledges that his formal musical training was limited. He is almost entirely self-taught. In fifth grade, when the opportunity to join the school band came along, he didn't think he would be good at playing an instrument, but the idea intrigued him. His grandfather encouraged him and bought him a plastic Conn clarinet at a local pawn shop. Dave learned all the Goodman classic tunes by listening to tapes and made his first public appearance at an elementary school concert playing *Bei Mir Bist Du Schoen*. By the age 10, he had decided that music would be his career.

Looking back, he states, "Prior to music, my main interest was drawing and artwork, and I wasn't listening to a lot of the music the other kids were into. When everyone heard I liked my grandparents' music, they looked at me like I had three heads. But once I played it for them, they really liked it."

At age 12, Dave was invited to New York to sit in with trumpet great Doc Cheatham at the Sweet Basil Jazz Club. In her early teens, he sent a tape to Pete Fountain, which resulted in an impromptu phone call from his idol, telling him that he was on the right track. At age 14, he started traveling to festivals with the New Reformation Jazz Band, an association that would continue for the next seven years.

At 17, he was selected one of two high school students from a field of 600 to perform as a special guest soloist with the Count Basie Orchestra. He premiered his *Tribute to Benny Goodman* septet in 2003 that resulted in his first feature CD of Goodman material. He joined the Hot Club of Detroit, a group that won the 2004 Heineken New Talent Search Award for their presentation of the music of Django Reinhardt-Stephane Grappelli's Hot Club of France.

From 2007 through 2009, he traveled the festival circuit with Wally's Warehouse Waifs. He made his European debut at the Bern International Jazz Festival in Switzerland in 2008. Since 2010, he has been performing with symphony orchestras throughout the United States and Canada, and 2013 saw him at Carnegie Hall with the New York Pops.

Dave's father built hot rod cars, so it's not surprising the son became a fan of Elvis Presley, Johnny Cash and Jerry Lee Lewis that led to forming a rockabilly band in high school and playing lots of hot licks on his classic Gretsch electric guitar. Of late, Dave has added a new fan base with his Memphis Speed Kings group that has become favorites of the swing dancers, playing classic 50s rock and roll while Dave emulates Jerry Lee Lewis with his wild gyrations at the piano, rollicking guitar and fast-paced vocals. He reports working on a new show that will offer a bit of Americana from swing to rock and roll.

Dave was always a good student in school, consistently bring home straight A's. At college, he opted to major in accounting and has both bachelor and master's degrees. He was been an avid weightlifter and was a powerlifter in his 20s.

The highly-respected Dick Hyman, who was the Goodman band touring pianist and music director of the final PBS Goodman feature, calls Dave Bennett "a phenomenon who plays his instrument beautifully, invents and improvises with great skill, and above all, in a perfect Benny Goodman manner, brings tremendous excitement to a performance."

Now at the ripe old age of 31, Dave modestly responds, "I've had a blessed career. The opportunities just seemed to come my way, for which I am most grateful. I manage to keep busy every day, and I'm happy to say I have bookings into early 2017. My faith keeps me grounded and I always try to be humble and not let success go to my head. I enjoy playing different styles of music, which is key to survival in today's musical environment. The bottom line is that I always try to give the fans a show they will enjoy and remember."

BRIAN CASSERLY
A Man of Many Hats

Published September 2015

Jazz fans know **Brian Casserly** as the charismatic leader of Cornet Chop Suey who wears a derby on stage and plays his horn one-handed.   Actually, Brian is a man of many hats, both past and present.

A professional musician since the age of 14, he is constantly in demand to play in bands that perform different musical genres, be it Dixieland, modern dance, rock, soul or blues. He is the musical director of MADCO (Modern American Dance Company) and was once the face of a campaign promoting St. Louis tourism. Trained as a pastry chef, he occasionally repairs instruments at St. Louis Woodwind and Brass for members of the St. Louis Symphony. *(No connection between the two; just an indication of his versatility.)*

So what's with the derby? A fan gave Brian a paper derby at a jam session, and he liked the effect it had on the audience so decided it would be one of his trademarks. It obviously took hold because on the occasion of his 52nd birthday celebration in 2012 at Joe's Café in St. Louis (known to its clientele as "the Poor Person's Country Club, Music Club and Miniature Golf Course"), everyone in attendance wore a black derby hat in honor of the birthday boy.

Playing the trumpet one-handed was another of those spur-of-the-moment things. When he was with the Soulard Blues Band, he alternated between playing lead trumpet and doing vocals. So he would play his horn holding it in his right hand and then reach for the microphone with his left hand when it came time to sing. So over time, he became comfortable being a one-arm trumpet player.

Brian recalls a concert at the University of Missouri where a gentleman seated in the front row kept saying, "Don't play that way." Brian later discovered it was the Mizzou band director who told him, "If my students saw you playing that way, they'd all come to class tomorrow trying to play one-handed."

Brian traces his ancestry back to Polish aristocracy and says his grandmother and grandfather sang in a Polish chorus at Carnegie Hall. Having settled in Long Island, New York, the family moved to St. Charles, Missouri when Brian was six, and his father, who was a banjo player, got a job in the McDonnell Douglas space program. Brian originally wanted to play the saxophone, but settled on the trumpet when a neighbor gave him the instrument. He played in jazz combos in high school as well as singing in vocal groups.

He attended the Stan Kenton Jazz Camp and joined the Musicians Union at 14. After high school, he decided to take a crack at the music scene in California where he played in a rock band and had the chance to perform with such notables as Tony Bennett, Tex Beneke and Tiny Tim. He enjoyed the freedom and the immediacy of doing well, but after a year, had to sell his horn to pay for a bus ticket back home.

He attended Southeast Missouri State University with the thought of becoming a doctor, but he decided music was his calling. In 1982, he joined Serapis, a rock band with horns that played Zappa, Steely Dan, Chicago and reggae. Three years later and for the next decade, he was music director of the S.S. Admiral, an excursion riverboat operating on the Mississippi River from the Port of St. Louis.

Having heard him with Bill Davis Dixieland band, Harry Opperman, a mainstay of the St. Louis Jazz Society, suggested Brian put a two-cornet band together to play at Society events, which became the genesis of Cornet Chop Suey. After much deliberation, the name for the band came from a tune written by Louis Armstrong and recorded by the Hot 5 in 1926. (Armstrong loved Chinese food and played both trumpet and cornet, although he preferred the trumpet for its more mellow tone. Cornet Chop Suey has the same configuration with Casserly on trumpet and Tom Tucker on cornet.)

It's a well-rehearsed and highly-entertaining show band that tours (sometimes as many as 18 concerts in 21 days) and is a popular draw at 12-15 festivals a year, plus a cruise.

As a member of the house band on the Goldenrod Showboat, a real 19th century riverboat, Brian can be found emulating Armstrong who blew lead notes on the river for Fate Marable's Society Syncopators 100 years ago. Brian directed the music for the premiered-presentation of "Liquid Roads," a 90-minute MADCO production celebrating St. Louis as a crossroads of music and featuring contemporary dance and live music inspired by New Orleans, Imperial Swing, steamboats and train travel. As he pointed out, "St. Louis has a tradition of being a crossroads with the river flowing north and south and the railroads coming from the east and west. All this brought people, and people brought their music."

With all his commitments, "Big B," a nickname picked up in high school, is out playing with local bands and various and sundry jams four or five nights a week when not on the road or plying the river. He enjoys being both a leader and sideman "because I know I'm among a bunch of great musicians playing the best music possible at that particular moment. It's what makes live music so special."

KATIE CAVERA
Always Sunny Side Up

Published July 2016

An indication of **Katie Cavera**'s popularity can easily be found by checking her calendar of upcoming engagements, which shows consistent bookings well into the future. She usually works three days a week with the Ellis Island Boys at Disneyland. For the past 16 years, she's had a Wednesday night sing-along gig with sousaphonist C.J. Sam's at Curley's Cafe in Long Beach. She works with a cabaret performance group called Vaud and the Villains, freelances with various groups at festivals, performs for swing dancers, and occasionally teaches at a jazz camp.

Her most notable qualities are her musicality, her versatility and her likeability. She's a rhythm guitar specialist in the style of Freddie Green and Al Casey, plays a hot 1920s plectrum and tenor banjo as well as a New Orleans-style string bass, and sings in the '20s pop style of Helen Kane and Ruth Etting. The late jazz critic Jim Leigh and bandleader/multi-instrumentalist Clint Baker dubbed her the "California Sunshine Girl" because of her ever-present sunny stage presence.

Growing up in Evansville, Indiana, Katie got a five-string banjo from her Dad at age 3, briefly took piano lessons, and had some exposure to bluegrass. She soon decided that the banjo was her instrument of choice, especially after hearing Clancy Hayes of the Lu Watters band.

It was off to Ball State University for two years before transferring to Indiana U. where she was a theater major and studied jazz performance and composition under Dr. David Baker, she credits for his guidance and encouragement. In addition to playing in a dixieland band, she was a member of Baker's jazz ensemble that performed a special presentation of Duke Ellington's Masterworks at the Smithsonian Institution in Washington, D.C.

She soon realized that a career in music would enable her to earn a living while having fun. It was while attending IU that she met Woody Pittman, a comedic magician. The couple were married for 20 years before Woody succumbed to kidney cancer in 2014. Katie learned some magic from her husband and is a member of the Academy of Magical Arts and Magic Castle, an exclusive club for magicians.

Moving to California in 1994, she freelanced, became a member of the San Fernando Banjo Band and over the years, worked with Jim Kweskin's Jug Band, Hal's Angels, Rhythm Rascals and the Reynolds brothers and appeared with jazz icons like Jim Cullum, Bob Helm, Bobby Gordon and Leon Oakley. In 2003, she traveled to Japan with Clint Baker's New Orleans Band that performed before an audience of 25,000 at the Jazz City Osaka Festival.

She considers George Probert, Clint Baker and Marc Caparone among her peers who became her mentors. Pianist Ray Skjelbred comments, "Katie loves what she does and makes everyone feel good about playing music with her. She's a timekeeper with a heartbeat sound." As drummer Hal Smith told her, "If a band can't play to your time, it can't play."

For a period of five years (2006-2011), she was part of a production, "A la Recherche de Josephine" *(Looking for Josephine),* a review about New Orleans jazz, Hurricane Katrina and Josephine Baker, with a score arranged by pianist David Boeddinghaus. The show premiered at the Opera Comique in Paris and subsequently toured Germany, Austria, Spain and France (plus an American premiere in Montclair, New Jersey). It was nominated for a Moliere Award, the national theater award bestowed by the Association Professionnelle et Artistique du Theatre.

Over the past dozen years, she along with several of her neighbors in the West Adams district of Los Angeles have been trapping feral cats and taking them to a local facility that will neuter them at no charge before releasing them where they no longer will be able to add to the overpopulation of these stray animals born in the wild.

EVAN CHRISTOPHER

Traveling the Clarinet Road

Published August 2017

Evan Christopher is passionate about two things: the style in which he plays his musical instrument, and the adopted city which he has called home since 1994. Based on the impact he has had on the world of music over the past quarter century, it should come as no surprise that the common denominator is New Orleans.

Alyn Shipton of the *London Jazz News* wrote: "If there is a better living exponent of the New Orleans Creole clarinet style than Evan Christopher, then it's a discovery I have yet to make." Critics remarking on his dynamic expressiveness and intimate approach have coined the phrase "close-encounter music." *The New York Times* called his respect for the music traditions of New Orleans "a triumph, joining the present seamlessly to a glorious past."

He travels on Clarinet Road as he strives to extend the legacies of the early Creole clarinetists: Sidney Bechet, Lorenzo Tio Jr., Omer Simeon, Barney Bigard and Albert Nicholas. Known as a meticulous researcher, he has identified certain stylistic traits that evolved from the work of early clarinetists that are part of the instrument's broad history in the Crescent City. He has identified a New Orleans clarinet vocabulary, which he has incorporated into his own style that has allowed him to produce a unique sound that looks to the future from the vantage of the past.

Originally from Long Beach, California, he acknowledges that his first musical instrument was a recorder. His experiments on the clarinet began at age 11, and he won the prestigious Louis Armstrong National Jazz Award while in high school. In his senior year, he met Marshall Hawkins at the Idyllwild Arts Academy in the San Bernadino mountains of Southern California. "Marshall Hawkins, who had played bass for Miles Davis, was my inspiration to continue my education. I knew I wanted to be a professional musician, but I needed to be reminded I had to stay on track"

He finished high school at the Idyllwild Arts Academy and went on to study saxophone with Dr. Thom Mason at the University of Southern California and got his music degree at Cal State-Long Beach, where he studied under Gary Bovyer and graduated cum laude. He gained experience playing with a number of area dixieland and swing bands, and in the early 1990s, went on tour with the singer-songwriter, A.J. Croce.

As Evan tells it, "I was on tour with A.J. Croce, and we passed through New Orleans. I had a few days off and met so many great musicians around my age playing traditional New Orleans jazz. They were very welcoming, and the protocols about sitting in and hanging out were very relaxed. It was unlike anything I had experienced before and seemed like the ideal place to go for what my interest was at the time. If you want to absorb a culture, a lifestyle and the history that makes a city what it is, you have to be there. That's why I made the move," which he did in 1994.

He spent nearly three years in San Antonio as the featured clarinetist with the Jim Cullum band and free-lanced for another year, but was back in the Big Easy in 2001. Four years later, Hurricane Katrina hit the city, and his Broadmoor neighborhood was flooded due to the failure of the Federal levees and floodwalls. He was not in New Orleans at the time of the storm, but nevertheless became one of approximately 4,000 displaced musicians. At the invitation of the French Government, he relocated to Paris where he formed two groups: The Jazz Traditions Project, a postmodern strategy that blurred the lines between genre and tradition, and Django a la Creole, that fused gypsy swing with New Orleans grooves and rhythm of "le monde Creole."

Tours with Irvin Mayfield's New Orleans Jazz Orchestra made it possible for Christopher to return to Louisiana where he has been permanently based since 2008. As a member of the adjunct faculty at the University of New Orleans, Evan coached a traditional New Orleans music ensemble for three semesters which had the distinction of being the only performing group at the university level dealing with New Orleans-style music.

How did he decide it was the Clarinet Road that he would travel? He disclosed that it was when he met Tony Scott, the late bebop clarinet player, and had him autograph a picture of himself taken backstage at Carnegie Hall with Charlie Parker and Billie Holiday. Scott signed it 'Good luck on Clarinet Road... lots of curves!'

Evan determined that "Tony gifted me that idea, and it seemed like a good way to describe what I do. I lost the poster in the flooding, but kept the Clarinet Road identity. The term can be the name of my band, a project, my publishing company, anything having to do with my career and all the curves it encompasses. There have been lots of curves, but the music will take care of you if you take care of it. You never know where it's going to lead you."

He has appeared twice at the venerable Newport Jazz Festival in Rhode Island. At the Satchmo Summerfest in New Orleans, he has given a talk on the music and lore of the famed Storyville District (2017 marked the 100th anniversary of its closing). He frequently returns to familiar territory for the Idyllwild Arts Jazz in the Pines fresh-air festival that was started by his mentor, Marshall Hawkins. He celebrated his 48th birthday at Le Duc Des Lombards, one of Paris's leading jazz clubs.

Ever the teacher, Jazz at Lincoln Center invited him to conduct a free, two-day workshop dealing with the current state of traditional New Orleans music. It also served as a refresher course covering the basic elements of early jazz. Calling his presentation, "Not Just Music for Dancers & Drinkers," he explained "Despite the music's humble beginnings and the commercial trappings that persist today, I attempted to lay out a framework to guide listeners towards a better understanding of the craft from the musician's perspective, which should encourage deeper listening skills that in turn, can help drive musical artistry."

Evan Christopher represents himself, does his own bookings and handles all the details that each performance demands. He's on the road about one-third of the time, but spends most of his time with his young family in New Orleans or in New York City. He constantly runs clinics, visits schools and gives master classes and private lessons as he continues to be an outspoken advocate for the preservation of early New Orleans jazz, not just through his music, but with education as well. (His website is *ClarinetRoad.com*.)

SHERRI COLBY & MATT BOTTEL
Tale of Two Cities

Published May 2014

*SherriLynn Colby and husband Matt Bottel are shown with
Their daughter Nevabelle in a 2014 photograph.*

Over the past 29 years, ***SherriLynn Colby-Bottel's*** career in jazz and education has come full circle, with the focus on two disparate communities: her hometown of Fresno, California and New Orleans. She was "discovered" at the age of 13 at a family gathering by newspaper columnist Woody Laughnan, who in short order, informed Forrest Helmick and Dave Ruffner that the newly-formed Blue Street Jazz Band had a vocalist.

On Wednesday nights for the next four years, Sherri's parents transported her to Blue Street rehearsals at Fresno High School and accompanied her when the band went on the road. In 1986, the band cruised the Mississippi River aboard the *Delta Queen* to New Orleans and made its first appearance at the Sacramento Jubilee. Sherri attended the Sacramento Traditional Jazz Society's summer camp for three summers where she met 14-year-old **Matt Bottel** whom she would marry 15 years later.

When Sherri graduated from Bullard High School, her parents allowed her to travel alone with the band, and the members took her under their collective protective wings. She went on to earn a Bachelor's degree in anthropology (1998) and a Master's in music (2001) at Fresno State University. Her Master's thesis dealt with the life stories of four current jazz singers: Yve Evans, Wende Harston, Sue Kroninger and Brady McKay. It was at Fresno State that Sherri developed a love for teaching when her academic mentor asked her to take over her classes, which she did for three years.

Her education continued at the University of Virginia in Charlottesville as a doctoral candidate in anthropology where she was named an outstanding graduate teaching assistant and received a National Science Foundation fellowship among several awards that enabled Sherri to earn her doctorate in 2012. Research on her doctoral dissertation took Sherri and Matt to Louisiana to examine the local management of traditional jazz in post-Katrina New Orleans.

When she received a UVA Faculty Senate dissertation-year fellowship for excellence in scholarship and teaching to assist in her final year of doctoral work at UV, she wrote: "Locals often explain traditional jazz as they explain the city: the culmination of centuries of blended peoples and cultures making New Orleans and its music unique. While 'cultural mixture' is credited in the development of New Orleans traditional jazz, that same music is now a century-long tradition – replete with expectations of historical authenticity and requirements of sincere musical engagement that must be upheld if the tradition is to be maintained."

"The stakes are high. The jazz iconography is a central element of New Orleans' tourism economy. It is also emblematic of a city where not so long ago, locals faced a disaster that sparked the fear of losing it all and becoming an inauthentic, corporatized caricature of itself."

- *Matt Bottel* -

When Matt Bottel was 9, his grandparents gave him a banjo for Christmas that they had purchased at an antique store. Two months later, he started taking lessons from Jack Martin in Sacramento that would continue for the next seven years. Matt recalls, "Jack was a terrific teacher who taught me a lot, but warned that I should not expect to make a living playing the instrument."

At age 10, he became a member of the Sacramento Banjo Band and gained the distinction of being the youngest musician to have performed at the annual Sacramento Jubilee up to that time. In 1985, he joined the Rocklin Quarry Cats, a group of junior and high school students who were regulars at the Jubilee for the next seven years.

He attended the STJS camp for four summers, and his grandparents would take him to festivals where Grandpa Stub Mattlin had no compunction in promoting his grandson and asking the leaders of performing bands if the young banjo player could sit in. In 1990, Matt entered California Polytechnic State University at San Luis Obispo as an engineering student, but graduated four years later with a degree in Industrial Technology. Throughout his college days he had a regular gig at a pizza parlor and also got to play with the Basin Street Regulars.

Not knowing for sure what he wanted to do professionally, he worked at a variety of jobs, joined the Cats 'n' Jammers jazz band led by Gene Berthelsen, and earned his Master's degree in Business Administration at Sacramento State. In 1997, both his Dad and Bob Williams of the Wooden Nickel Jazz Band were working at Electronic Data Systems and urged Matt to apply for an apprentice system engineer position. In spite of not having any experience, he was hired, saying "EDS actually had a policy of hiring musicians and artists as they found them to make good engineers and programmers."

The Sacramento EDS office had several musicians on staff, and Matt joined Williams, Paul Edgerton and Tom Lopes to form Ed's Quartet. They played for company functions and at nearby wineries, prompting Matt to say, "There's nothing like getting paid with a case of great California wine."

While remaining friends over the years, that summer camp friendship picked up in late 1999. Sherri and Matt became formally engaged on Tax Day 2001 and were married on September 29, 2001, with Dave Ruffner officiating. That year, Matt became an official member of the Blue Street Jazz Band, replacing Robert Bennett, the band's original banjo man. When Sherri and Matt moved to Virginia in 2003, EDS allowed Matt to become a full-time telecommuter and has since continued to work at home. He is now a 15-year veteran in systems engineering and leads a team of engineers, designers and programmers who work on large-scale projects with national implications.

Matt had his first gig four days after moving to New Orleans and maintained a busy performing schedule playing clubs, jazz brunches, private parties, riverboats and corporate events. Looking back, he said, "There is no other place in the world like New Orleans where 10 full-time banjo players and another five part-timers could all make a living."

Now a faculty member at Fresno State, Dr. SherriLynn Colby-Bottel has had a fulfilling career in her young life to date, combining a great love of music and her academic work as an anthropologist. "Anthropology is the science of what it is to be human, understanding the world in which we live," she states. "Recognizing what has happened in New Orleans over the past decade, how the city responded to a major catastrophe, and how music, specifically traditional jazz, played a major role as the city struggled to reclaim its heritage is a fascinating story."

"The culture of New Orleans is the people. It is the hallmark of the city. In many ways, New Orleans is different than the rest of the United States. New Orleans has always been a port city with constant comings and goings. People came back after Katrina because of their commitment to the city. A new generation of young musicians have settled in New Orleans, seeking to live an authentic life. Many are working on street corners for tips and surviving. It has become cool to be 'old-timey'."

"Traditional New Orleans jazz is having a renaissance in the Big Easy. The music may not sound like it did in 1917 or 1929, but we are drawing from a whole century of sounds. Traditional jazz is a real living thing, not a historic relic. It is constantly changing, making for enjoyment in many ways."

"In some respects, it is a backlash against the Digital Age. It counters the non-tactile coldness of much of what is so impersonal in today's society, filling the void and need for social contact and doing something together."

ADRIAN CUNNINGHAM
A Talent from Down Under

Published June 2917

Australian-born **Adrian Cunningham** got hooked on jazz early in life listening to his father's collection of Big Band recordings. As he began to achieve success early in his career in his native country, he realized that if he wanted to play American jazz, he should live in America and to be part of the culture of the people that created the music.

Following graduation from the Sydney Conservatory of Music with a degree in Performance in Jazz Clarinet, he organized and toured with his own band, was a member of the famous Galapagos Duck and the Sydney All-Star Big Band, and played at the prestigious Montreux Jazz Festival in Switzerland.

One of Adrian's college professors recommended that he take lessons from Grammy Award-winning clarinetist Eddie Daniels, who is considered a virtuoso in both jazz and classical music and who formerly played with the Thad Jones/Mel Lewis Orchestra. Adrian did so on two occasions at Daniels' home in New Mexico.

Adrian visited New York City in 2007, primarily as a tourist, but also to check out the local jazz scene and get a few lessons. He was so inspired that when he returned to Sydney, he realized he probably would never play at the level he heard in the Big Apple living in Australia. "I knew I just had to give it a try, or I would regret it for the rest of my life. I needed to make that connection."

The transition was not easy in trying to establish himself in a highly-competitive music environment. "It was tough, but challenging. It was important to make the most of every opportunity and to follow through with every contact I was able to make. In my first week, I was looking for a room to rent and checked out a place in Brooklyn. It turned out that the guy living there was a musician, and we got to talking. He invited me to sit in on his gig that Saturday night, and I subsequently joined the band for what became my first regular Saturday night gig."

"I would go busking in Central Park three or four days a week and met some great people. It was quite a humbling experience playing for tips in front of people like Alec Baldwin, Owen Wilson and Keith Jarrett. But I was fortunate in finding work very quickly in the traditional jazz scene with a whole generation of young musicians who were reviving the music. I also connected with some of the more established musicians like Ed Polcer who were helpful in my getting established in a new city."

He soon was performing at all the top jazz clubs: Blue Note, Birdland, Smalls, Dizzy's Club at Lincoln Center and the Village Vanguard. For two years, he was the leader of the saxophone section of Vince Giordano's Nighthawks, which he called "a real education in traditional jazz." He formed his own New Orleans-style band: Professor Cunningham and His Old School, which has become one of the top groups in the international Swing scene, garnering numerous awards along the way.

Explaining how he settled on the name of his band, "Since the band was playing traditional rather than commentary music, I wanted to distinguish it from my more modern or original music. So I thought. . .old music. . .old school. Then I thought. . .old school...teacher...professor! And the rest is history."

"I've been fortunate to play with some wonderful people in all sorts of situations. I played the Montreux Festival two years in a row with blues singer Sweet George Brown. Recently I've been touring and recording with trombonist Wycliffe Gordon, whom I consider the closest horn player to Louis Armstrong. In one of those surreal moments, I did a big band gig with trumpet legend Lew Soloff (formerly of Blood, Sweat & Tears), for which we were each paid $30."

"I got to play Carnegie Hall in 2016 where I performed one of my own tunes with the New York Concerti Sinfonietta. I'm happy going up to the American Legion Hall in Harlem and playing for all those swing dancers. It blows my mind when I see 100 young people dancing to the music of Duke Ellington."

His instruments have been described as "a breathy tenor sax, fluid clarinet and cirrus-sounding flute." As to his favorite, he responds, "It's like asking a parent which is his favorite child. I choose the instrument according to the song. The saxophone – and he plays both tenor and alto – is definitely the most prolific of the woodwinds at the moment. The clarinet requires a stricter technique than the sax as well as greater discipline and more practice to get it sounding good. The flute has been present in jazz since the early days, but not as a major voice."

"Each instrument has a unique quality and character that I love to explore. When I pick up the flute, I am a flute player, not a saxophone player who plays the flute. When it comes to recording, I much prefer live recordings which have a very special quality to them; a spontaneity and energy not often found in a studio setting. I want to capture the heat of the moment."

Adrian enjoys composing heart-warming songs by reflecting on the emotions he has felt through a variety of life experiences, which in turn, he feels allows his audience to share these emotions as they listen to him play. A promo for the artist stated, "Adrian Cunningham has the incredible ability to paint a musical picture and capture the energy of the moment with his melodic songwriting and improvisation." His songs have twice been featured in the in-flight program on Qantas Airline domestic and international flights as well as on radio stations in Australia.

It's all happened in a little over 10 years since this Aussie transplant landed on America's shores. While he spends over half his time performing overseas, the United States has become his home base. He sums up what he has accomplished over the past decade, saying, "Success is a series of small steps. Each year provides more opportunities and forges new relationships. I don't really have a master plan as to where I'm headed. I just want to be the best that I can."

EDDIE ERICKSON
The Good Humor Man

Published November 2014

Eddie Erickson – virtuoso banjoist and guitarist, vocal stylist and entertaining showman – has to be one of the most affable and approachable musicians on the jazz circuit today.

He was born in San Francisco in 1948 and grew up in nearby Santa Clara. His father played the guitar "for his own amazement," according to Eddie. "His sense of time wasn't very good. We had a neighbor who played the ukulele, so I decided to take up the uke at the age of seven. But I soon got bored and shot holes in the instrument with my bb gun."

"At 13, I saw a banjo in a music store, but was told it was too expensive. That Christmas, I received a tenor banjo my parents purchased with a half-down payment, with the stipulation I pay the remaining half from my newspaper route earnings and take lessons. My teacher was a Filipino gentleman who spoke little English. After three months, we parted ways. I got a couple books and records of George Van Eps and Louis Armstrong and began teaching myself. After hearing Eddie Peabody and Perry Bechtel, I became inspired." Django Reinhardt, Joe Pass, Wes Montgomery and Howard Roberts are other guitarists who have had an influence on his playing.

When he was 15, Eddie got his first professional job playing for free in a local pizza parlor, but he was fired after two weeks when it was discovered he was underage. Two years later, he switched to the plectrum banjo and developed an interested in the guitar.

This led to his first steady job in 1968 at the famous and colorful Capone's Warehouse on Cannery Row in Monterey where he added cornet to his repertoire. "It was a family joint that had evolved into a nightclub. It was usually a free-for-all where anything was apt to happen. But for me, it was like a university for learning about show business and being an entertainer. We did a lot of Spike Jones routines, and I even had a guitar shaped like a toilet seat. The waitresses were called 'The Untouchables,' and I ended up marrying one."

He next headed for Disney World and Disneyland where he was featured in the Class of '27 Show at the Diamond and Golden Horseshoes and also performed with the Banjo Kings. From 1978 to 1983, he led the Riverboat Rascals show band on board the Empress Lilly Showboat. "We played six nights a week in a boat set in cement in a shopping mall that was surrounded by Lake Buena." It was back to Monterey in 1984 where he hooked up with Jackie Coon and the Abalone Stompers.

His growing reputation in the jazz community soon earned him work and recordings with such luminaries as Rick Fay, Bucky Pizzarelli, Johnny Varro, Dick Hyman, Dave Frishberg, Big Mama Sue Kroninger and many others. In 2000, he became part of the Becky

73

Kilgore Quartet that included Dan Barrett and Joel Forbes. He began getting invited to the elite jazz parties and traveled overseas. In 2006, he was recognized as the Musician of the Year at the Sweet & Hot Festival in Los Angeles. For the past 20 years, Eddie has shared his seasoned skills with youth camps and workshops and finds this highly rewarding and important in keeping jazz alive.

Like Fats Waller, Eddie expressed concern that some people may view his display of humor while performing as overriding his consummate desire to be seen as a serious musician. "I take my performing very seriously and always aim to please the audience," he said. "But I may too often put undue pressure on myself in spite of outward appearances.I genuinely enjoy interacting with people, but the travel, performing, long hours and non-stop socializing can be exhausting and somewhat stressful. When I return home to Pacific Grove, California, I find I need a few days to recharge my battery."

In spite of his reservations, Eddie is held in extremely high regard by his peers. Noting that he has a great natural ear, musically speaking, Becky Kilgore says, "If he doesn't know the tune, he is very quick in figuring out the chords." Dan Barrett chimed in, "Eddie has great tone and is technically adept at providing just the right time and rhythm. He phrases like a trumpet player and constantly demonstrates the ability to mix good humor with top-flight music while not diminishing his musicality."

His many fans will take issue when he says he doesn't feel like a professional musician or consider himself a great singer. His website refers to him as "Fast Eddie" and "The Singing Moustache." His business card reads, "Yesterday's music at today's prices." When asked how he wants people to view him, he modestly responds, "I'm just a guy who plays music."

THE FOUR FRESHMEN

Always in Harmony

Published April 2017

In an era of ever-changing musical styles and tastes, it's truly amazing that **The Four Freshmen** have been harmonizing, recording and touring for 69 years, certainly qualifying them as the longest continuously performing quartet of its kind in the United States.

It was in early 1948 that brothers Ross and Don Barbour, then students at Butler University's Arthur Jordan Conservatory of Music in Indianapolis, Indiana, formed a barbershop quartet (along with Hal Kratzch and Marvin Pruitt) called Hal's Harmonizers. They wore false mustaches, armbands and waiters' aprons and sang Gay 90s tunes like *Sweet Adeline* and *In the Shade of the Old Apple Tree*.

It wasn't long before they became bored with that routine, but didn't want to give up the income. So they form a second group – The Toppers - to experiment with more complex chords and jazzier arrangements patterned after The Modernaires of the Glenn Miller Orchestra and Mel Torme's Mel-Tones. Their popularity grew as they performed at college events, local malt shops and bars, but it resulted in a casualty: Marvin Pruitt developed acute stage fright and left the group.

He was initially replaced by Ross Barbour's girlfriend, but it was decided a fourth male voice would be more appropriate for the sound they were trying to develop. Bob Flanigan, a cousin of the Barbours who played the trombone and had excellent pitch and phrasing, was recruited to take over as the male lead.

They rehearsed in a parked car with the windows closed to work out their own unique style of improvised vocal harmony. They signed with an agent who suggested Freshmen Four as a name, but they reversed the words and went on the road in September 1948 with

Flanigan (1st tenor) and Kratzch (bass) alternating between brass and string bass; Ross Barbour (baritone) moving from piano to drums; and brother Don (2nd tenor) continuing to play guitar.

There were nights when they earned as little as $5 in tips, but they began to get the attention of people like Woody Herman and Dizzy Gillespie. Their big break came in 1950 when bandleader Stan Kenton, who had been told that there was a quartet in town that "sounded like his 43-piece ensemble," went to hear them at the Esquire Lounge in Dayton, Ohio. He was sufficiently impressed to arrange an audition with Capitol Records, who signed them later that year.

Their sound has been characterized by long, lush chords – Ross Barbour called them "purple chords" – and an improvisational style that made four voices seem like five or six. Bob Flanigan was quoted as saying, "We all thought in instrumental terms like horn players. I approached singing lead as if I was playing the trombone in Stan Kenton's band. We also use no vibrato because Kenton's trombones didn't."

It's a Blue World, their first big hit, was first recorded in 1952 and has been their most requested tune over the years. It is included in just about every concert along with such standards as *Day by Day, The Day Isn't Long Enough, Poinciana, Laura* and *Graduation Day*. Their top-selling album has been *The Four Freshmen & Five Trombones*. Dick Reynolds, Pete Rugolo and several former and current members of the group have done the arrangements.

Brian Wilson, the leader and co-founder of the Beach Boys, was inspired by the Four Freshmen, calling them his "harmonic education." The Freshmen are also credited with influencing the styles of such groups as The Lettermen, Four Preps, Manhattan Transfer, and the Mamas and Papas.

Traditional jazz festivalgoers are familiar with the Four Freshmen songbook, thanks to the Sorta/Kinda Dixie Jazz Band from Las Vegas. When Jim Fitzgerald was forming the group, they discovered an affinity for four-part vocals, particularly those by the Four Freshmen and the Ink Spots. One day they were rehearsing, and Autie Goodman, one of the Freshmen, walked in with a stack of charts, which he presented to Jim with the admonition, "If you're going to do our songs, you might as well get them right."

Over the years, the Freshmen have recorded 50 albums and received six Grammy nominations. *Downbeat Magazine* named them the best vocal group five times, and they were inducted into the Vocal Group Hall of Fame in 2001.

Bob Flanigan had the longest tenure of the original Freshmen – 44 years – and continued to manage the group for five years until his death in 2011. Over the nearly seven decades, some 26 vocalists-instrumentalists have taken the stage as one of the Four Freshmen.

The current aggregation - #25 – is headed by Bob Ferreira, who has been with the group for the past 24 years, having joined while a music student at Central Washington University. During his tenure, he has performed in all 50 states and 10 foreign countries and been the drummer on nine Four Freshmen recordings. The others are Stein Malvey, who has a degree in guitar performance from Lawrence University Conservatory of Music in Appleton, Wisconsin; Tommy Boynton on string bass, a graduate of the New England Conservatory in Boston, Mass.; and newcomer Jon Gaines, another product of the New England Conservatory, who plays trumpet and flugelhorn.

2019 Four Freshmen: Tommy Boynton, Jonathan Gains, Bob Ferreira, Stein Malvey

The Freshmen do 80 shows a year and usually are on the road for 10 days to two weeks at a stretch before having a break. "There are times when it can be a demanding schedule," according to Ferreira. "As an example, after packing up following a 7:30pm concert in Scottsdale, Arizona, we drove six hours to Vista, California, *arriving* at 4:30am. We were up at 8:30am for a 2pm concert, to be followed by another at 7pm. It's important that we learn to pace ourselves and to stay healthy, as we rarely use substitutes. I once played for over a month while getting over whopping cough."

When Curtis Calderon announced that he would be leaving the group at the end of 2016 to spend more time with his growing family, the search was on to find a replacement, which ended up being Jon Gaines. Ferreira then sent six charts of the Four Freshmen's most popular tunes so that Jon could learn the third vocal part. Then it was another six charts and another six, followed by a week of rehearsals with the other three musicians until Jon was comfortable with the three dozen most popular songs that the group does before going out on the road. "We don't refer to charts when we play, so it all has to memorized – from vocals to solos to breaks. It happens pretty fast, and any new member has to quickly grasp the Four Freshmen sound and style."

The entire Four Freshmen library involving hundreds of charts is currently being archived at Butler University. Whenever their schedule allows, the Freshmen will do workshops and master classes for aspiring musicians. "You have to reach young people at an early age in order to make a lasting impression," Bob Ferreira points out. "We also use social media to reach the younger audience."

The Four Freshmen still have a loyal following, with a fan club of 3,000 members that holds an annual convention. "The members are not just fans; they have become friends" in Bob Ferreira's opinion. "We always strive to do justice to these wonderful tunes. The music has impact and meaning to each and everyone in the audience. The songs have evolved from life experiences and are timeless."

The name of this long-lasting vocal group may be indicative of some kind of premonition because none of the original Freshmen graduated from college, although Bob Flanigan and Ross Barbour did receive honorary degrees from Butler. They will just remain Four Freshmen forever.

THE HEITGERS

Duke and Ray

Published October 2013

Duke Heitger has been a New Orleans-based musician for the past 22 years. Just out of college he was invited to join Jacques Gauthe's Creole Rice Jazz Band in 1991 at the age 22, an association that lasted five years. He took over Eddie Bayard's Steamboat Stompers and has since headed the group's twice-daily cruises on the Mississippi River aboard the paddlewheeler Natchez. He's toured with Banu Gilson, performed extensively in Europe, and has a platinum record on the wall of his Uptown apartment for being the unseen trumpet player on the Squirrel Nut Zippers' 1997 release, *Hot*.

Duke Heitger

Duke grew up in a jazz-loving family, saying "My father Ray loved New Orleans jazz, and I got to hear recordings of the Masters - Armstrong, Berigan, Hackett and Beiderbecke - at a very early age. I was never pushed into liking or playing this music. It was more that my family provided an avenue into appreciating traditional jazz, and I was able to discover it at my own pace. I was fortunate to have grown up in this environment."

He originally thought he might play the clarinet like his father, but switched to the trumpet. He knew eight songs at the age of nine – all in B flat, and by 12, he was sitting in with Ray's Cakewalkin' Jass Band. What truly inspired him to become a musician was hearing a young Jon-Erik Kellso, who was four years older, and then telling his Dad, "When I'm 17, I should be able to play that well." It wasn't long before he knew 250 tunes.

Duke paid his way through prep school (where he had a Dixieland band) and college (where he majored in geology) with what he earned as a young musician. Jacques Gauthe heard Duke at the Central City Colorado Festival in 1990 and offered him a job. But Duke deferred until he graduated from the University of Toledo. Even after moving to the Big Easy, he continued his education, earning a Master's degree in geology at the University of New Orleans in 2006, but has yet to work a day as a geologist.

When the Squirrel Nut Zippers, known for their eclectic fusion of Delta blues, gypsy jazz, 1930s swing and klezmer, came to New Orleans in 1997 to make a record, they were in need of a horn player and hired Duke sight unseen. After a day of recording, they begged him to join the group, but he declined. *Hot* went on to become a platinum record with sales in excess of a million and a half. The MTV video for the hit single acknowledges Duke on a lengthy solo, showing a disembodied trumpet by itself, spiraling crazily through the air.

"Do I regret not going with the Zippers?" Duke reflects. "That's not what I do musically, and certainly it's a different lifestyle. The Zippers were popular for a few years, but in the long run, I'm better off. But it was really neat to have been a small part of pop culture for just a little while."

Duke says his job on the Nachez is anything but routine and definitely not a matter of just regurgitating old favorites. "We're drawing from over a thousand tunes, easily," he contends. "These are such great tunes, gems that you hardly hear anymore. When we introduce some of these melodies to the hippest of crowds, they just love them."

In addition, Duke travels to Europe one week a month and can be heard at the Palm Court Jazz Café and Preservation Hall as well as performing at occasional private parties and conventions. He's been on Garrison Keillor's *A Prairie Home Companion* program as well as Jim Cullum's Riverwalk Jazz broadcasts. For a brief time, he even provided the musical background for the Shim Shamettes burlesque performances.

The Patriarch: Ray Heitger -
Ray Heitger didn't pick up a musical instrument until he was 19 years old. "I had friends who were musicians, and it struck me that they were having fun, so I decided to give it a try," he recalled. "I've always been a self-taught musician and don't read music, always playing by ear." Listening to a Kid Ory recording sold him on New Orleans-style jazz.

He organized the New Orleans Footwarmers in 1963, followed by a five-piece band that he called "Dixieland 5½, giving credit to the banjo player for playing both banjo and cornet. The Cakewalkin' Jass Band with four members came into being in 1967, and a year later were hired for twice-weekly gigs at Tony Packo's Café, a Hungarian-style restaurant in Toledo, an engagement that lasted nearly 33 years.

"Packo's wasn't a real jazz club, but more of an atmosphere place," Ray said. "Everything just clicked, with a lot of dancing and audience participation. We drew people of all ages, and a party atmosphere prevailed. Everyone enjoyed the fun we were having. But by 2002, the club scene had changed, and there was too much alternative entertainment. So ended one of the longest-running gigs in the history of jazz."

The Cakewalkers played 17 consecutive Bix Beiderbecke Memorial Festivals and are still a hard-driving band after 46 years, thanks to the efforts of 29 full-time members (only five of whom performed on the front line) and 51 substitute musicians. The band, which can number between four and eight depending on the occasion, still does festivals and local events. Ray is retired after a 47-year career as a mathematics instructor at several Midwestern universities. He travels to Ann Arbor for a weekly gig with a trio which draws a younger audience anxious learn about classic jazz.

Jazz has been a true family experience for the Heitgers, who for a brief period, even had a family band. "My wife Betty played piano, although she could only play chords," according to Ray. "Our oldest daughter Renee played the gutbucket; our second daughter Andrea was on guitar; and our youngest, Nicole, who now is the vocalist for the Cakewalkers, played the snare drum at age 6." While Betty admitted her musical skills were limited, she said she has thoroughly enjoyed 46 years of great memories and making countless friends.

BRIAN HOLLAND

Predestined to Perform

Published 2018

Brian Holland feels that his career as a professional musician was preordained. His music existence began at the age of 3. Blessed with perfect pitch and an aptitude for improvisation, he learned his way around an organ keyboard and had a repertoire of old standards – all before the age of 6. He was playing four nights a week at a local inn between the ages of 12 and 14. He is the youngest person to win the World Old-Time Piano-Playing Championship, not once but three times, with the third title coming at age 27.

Classically-trained, Brian has been performing jazz, ragtime and stride piano for 35 years. His approach to the piano is marked by a dynamic, driving style that has been described as "clear as Waterford crystal." Constantly developing new and exciting styles of performance, he continues to enthrall audiences by combining impressively dexterous pyrotechnics with a laid-back approach, seemingly with little or no effort.

But Brian is not willing to rest on past laurels. "What is most important in music is to never stop learning, to always be open to experiencing and absorbing new things, to always work to improve what you are doing. It's continual on-the-job training.

Brian's father was in the Air Force and therefore constantly on the move. So young Brian was raised by his grandparents who lived in Indianapolis, Indiana. They taught him to appreciate all kinds of music, especially styles from the turn of the 20th century. His grandfather had an electric Lowrey organ, so by the age of 3, Brian was picking out notes and eventually playing simple jingles he heard on television.

Brian loves to tell the story about the time when he was still hardly able to reach the pedals of the organ that his mother called her mother and could hear the organ being played in the background. The grandmother asked, "Do you know who that is?" Brian's mother responded, "Oh, yes. That's Dad," to which Grandma replied, "No, that's your son!"

By age 6, he was taking lessons on the organ and practicing four hours a day, which became his regiment for the next dozen years. It was at about this time in his life that it became apparent that music was his overriding interest. "Music was always there, so there was no question as to the direction in which I was headed," he recalled.

He had his first professional gig at age 7 when his grandfather took him to a local music store that sold organs. The store had brought in two traveling artists to demonstrate a brand-new organ and put on a concert. As Brian recounts the story, "Naturally they were trying to sell the new organ and talked about how easy it was to play. They had me in the audience as a plant. As they were making their pitch, they motioned to me and said, 'You in the front row, you, little kid. Why don't you come up and show everybody how easy it is to play this organ? So I got up and played a song on the organ. They paid me 50 bucks."

He became proficient on the piano, studying under a German lady who played in the Indianapolis Symphony Orchestra, which gave him an extensive background in the Classics. He joined the Musicians Union at the age of 12 and was hired to play four nights a week at the famed Boggstown Inn & Cabaret, which is located 20 miles southeast of downtown Indianapolis.

Brian describes the Inn as "being in the middle of a cornfield" in a community that had a population of around 400 at the time. The town's most famous resident was Marjorie Main (1890-1975), who appeared in 82 films and is best remembered as Ma Kettle. The building that houses the Cabaret (now known as the BC Supper Club) was built in 1873 and housed the first Red Man's Lodge in Indiana. It was situated next to the Seventh Day Adventist Home for Unwed Mothers and for many years was Boggstown's general store and barber shop. From its opening in 1984, the Cabaret was the site of many Hoosier Ragtime Society gatherings and provided musicians the opportunity to tell stories and jokes in a down-home setting that had a burlap-covered backdrop and picnic-style seating and to play their favorite ragtime tunes.

In high school, Brian played the saxophone in school bands and orchestras, after which he spent a period of time playing majestic pipe organs in pizza parlors. Needing to earn some money between gigs, he entered the field of retail store management in the early 1990s, which became his primary livelihood for the next 22 years. But music was always there. As spare-time bookings and recordings picked up, he realized he was only truly happy when he was seated at the piano. It was at the urging of his wife that he decided to become a full-time musician on January 15, 2015 at the age of 42.

In 1997, Brian met Jeff Barnhart at the Scott Joplin International Ragtime Festival in Sedalia, Missouri. At an after-hours session, Brian and Jeff decided to try a couple of well-received piano duets, which led to an all-night jam session that didn't end until 8 a.m. the next morning. It was obvious that they were on to something special in how their styles meshed, with Jeff's take-no-prisoners approach, and Brian's more laid-back classical take on ragtime and jazz. The two have recorded three CDs. (Brian has since served as artistic director of the Joplin Festival beginning in 2015.)

Even as a part-time musician, Brian had an off-season job in Atlantic City at the Showboat Casino, garnered a Grammy nomination for his work with Bud Dresser (trombone-tuba-vocals) on their album, *Ragtime-Goodtime-Jazz,* and took his unique styling to the International Stride Summit in Zurich, Switzerland in 2007. He calls the 2010 opportunity to play in Rwanda, Africa and tour the countryside with drummer Danny Coots "a life-changing experience." The two performed before sold-out crowds at the first Buenos Aires, Argentina Ragtime Festival in 2014.

The Coots-Holland musical partnership has resulted in eight recordings, festival bookings and annual tours in the United States. As a record company executive explained, "Holland and Coots take you on a musical journey that radiates joyful ebullience one moment and wistful lyricism the next." A faculty member at the Eastman School of Music observed, "They should come with seat belts and a warning about excessive amounts of white-knuckle, adrenaline-charge, exuberant effervescence."

Danny Coots gives his take on the relationship, writing: "I started a project some years ago to study how, as a drummer and accompanist, my playing would have to adjust and change depending on the people with whom I was playing. I found that the opportunity to play with just piano players was not only musically very interesting, but was a blast."

"When Brian Holland and I first played together, I realized we were onto something very special. His background in classical music and years of a solid work ethic led technique way beyond the crowd. His interest in many styles and ability to create in the moment was right down my alley. I've learned that a musician plays who he is. His music is always open, creative and generous. The Holland/Coots Duo is one of the highlights of my career."

In his 44 years, Brian Holland has covered a lot of ground, played a lot of notes, and had some great experiences in playing the music he loves. He concluded our conversation observing, "A friend of mine once said that the only way to become a millionaire playing the kind of music that I do is to start off with two million dollars and work your way backwards. We don't do it for money; we do it because we love it."

TOM HOOK

A Love of Music and History

Published September 2013

The desire to be a performing musician and a consuming love of history, especially as related to the Mississippi River, have been the primary driving forces in **Tom Hook**'s career as the consummate musician. Born in Kansas City, he grew up in the hills of Northern Missouri, saying "We were country folks and were always having hootenannies where we would play and sing old-time folk music. From the age of three, I can't remember when I didn't play the piano."

Born with perfect pitch, he didn't take lessons until he was 8. He played trombone in his school marching band and jazz band, was active in school theater productions, and dabbled with the guitar, mandolin and 5-string banjo. He began his career in 1970 performing in local and regional jazz and rock bands. It was with a Dixieland band at the World of Fun theme park in Kansas City where "the older musicians really taught me about jazz." He composed his first song at age 17.

"I knew I always wanted to be a musician and to play and appreciate every style," he states. "While I would say that Teddy Wilson is my favorite piano player, Fats Waller was in many ways my inspiration as a musician and entertainer. I love the goofiness he projected, but I always try to strike the proper balance between music and entertainment. Louis Armstrong, Nat King Cole, Louis Jordan and Louis Prima are among the singers I admire."

Graduating from high school in 1974, he worked at various jobs and became a founding member of the New Red Onion Jazz Babies, a popular traditional jazz band, playing banjo. In 1980 he began a 30-year association with the Delta Queen Steamboat Company. Starting out as a lounge entertainer on board the Mississippi Queen, he became the bandleader on Delta Queen in 1984 where he had the opportunity to work with folk and bluegrass songwriter-entertainer John Hartford whose relatively short career and music were shaped by his experiences as a performer and pilot on the Mississippi River. (Hartford composed *Gentle on My Mind* which was later popularized by Glen Campbell.)

Tom said he only left the river when something better came along, plus the need to spend more time with his growing family. He always had the desire to be a Disney musician, so in 1986, a call to Bill Allred took him to Orlando, Florida as a staff musician at Rosie O'Grady's at the popular Church Street Station. His job at Church Street spring-boarded him into a full-time position as a staff musician at Disney World. He soon had his own vintage rock band, The Terrier Brothers, that included Bobby Durham and Ed Metz Jr. With a regular gig at Orchid Garden, they also became the relief band at Lil' Darlin's Rock and Roll Place in Kissimmee where they appeared with many of the rock legends from the 1950s and 60s.

It was in 1987 that trombonist Steve Yokum recruited a group of Disney staff musicians to make a cassette which was released as *Come Hear the Truth*. They didn't think much would happen with the band after that, but a few copies of the CD were sent to festival directors which got them their first jobs at the Suncoast and Bix Beiderbecke festivals in 1989. The Black Dogs soon took the festival circuit by storm with their unique fusion of New Orleans Second Line, Swamp Jazz, Zydeco and Jump Swing

Drummer Ed Metz recalls, "We were all very excited that the band was taking off and had visions of hitting it big. We talked about putting together a giant show like a rock band. We didn't sound like anyone else, and we felt we could be the band to breach the generation gap. We did a lot of improvising on the bandstand.

Sometimes half the band would be headed one way on a number, and the other half was off in another direction. We'd ask ourselves 'how do we get out of this mess?' and we'd usually end up with a drum solo."

In 1991-92, the Dogs appeared at 36 festivals, a killing pace that began to affect their personal lives. There were multiple trips to Europe as well as a 1989 tour of Communist China. The group continued in various configurations with Hook as leader until they made their final appearance at the Breda Holland Festival in 2012.

The 1990s saw Tom portraying Sam the Bartender at the Diamond Horseshoe in Disney World, spending time as music director at the Main Street Station Casino in Las Vegas and returning to the riverboats as staff musician and bandleader. In 1999, he returned to MGM Studios in Orlando, and was on the opening staff for Pat O'Brien's nightclub on Universal Studio City Walk at Disney World where he received the coveted "Golden Woody" awarded annually to City Walk's premier entertainer.

In 2000 Tom began working as Manager of Entertainment for the six ships of the Delta Queen Steamship Company, with a brief hiatus as Music Director at Harrah's Casino New Orleans due to Delta Queen's bankruptcy following the September 11, 2001 bombing of the World Trade Center. In 2002, he returned as Director of Entertainment for the restructured steamboat line, now run by Delaware North Companies. In 2007, he formed Daymark Productions to produce and administer entertainment for the six ships of the Majestic America Line. He currently is Musical Director for Cruise Artistes International and does about six jazz festivals a year on his own or with the reconstituted Terrier Brothers..

He has been a guest artist many times on Jazzdagen Tours which has taken him all over the world. He has been to Malaysia with the Garden District Trio and makes annual tours to Japan with Tom Fischer's New Orleans Jazz All-Stars. He's been the voice talent on jingles for Budweiser, McDonald's, H&R Block and Kansas City Chiefs. His one-man stage production of *Riverman* about a 19th century riverboat pilot brings some of the most powerful and poignant events of that period in the country's history to light through original songs, carefully researched stories and photographs. He performs *Riverman* regularly on board the vessels of American Cruise Lines.

Tom considers himself "a real history nut," and his latest venture has taken him into the world of cyber entertainment where he has been involved in producing and recording period music for a series of computerized war games developed by John Tiller for HPS

Simulations that cover 55 different military campaigns ranging from the Ancient Roman Wars up through the 20th Century.

"It's been a real challenge because the music from those early days was played on different instruments and had different sounds," he says. "I've had to do considerable research to get a feeling and sense of what that sound might be. One conclusion I've come to is that we lived in a much quieter world before the 20th Century."

Back home in New Orleans, Tom can be heard performing at Houston's Restaurant on St. Charles Avenue, Dos Jefes Uptown Cigar Bar, Fritzel's European Jazz Pub at 733 Bourbon Street (the city's oldest continuously-operating jazz club), the Royal Orleans Hotel or the Carousel Bar at the Monteleone Hotel. In addition, he makes frequent "step-on" appearances on board the American Queen and Queen of the Mississippi riverboats with his own All-Star ensemble featuring New Orleans trumpet great Wendell Brunious. He extols, "The music scene in New Orleans is exploding, and there is more work to be had here than before Katrina. I'm working seven nights a week, playing different styles, and couldn't be happier. New Orleans today is all about music."

As Tom sums it up, "I'm a guy who loves American popular music in all its forms and who desires to share as much of the joy and sadness that is inherent in this music with as many people as possible."

.

JON-ERIK KELLSO
A Propitious Phone Call

Published May 2015

Sometimes life's opportunities are due to a stroke of luck or a flip of a coin. Or it could just be a matter of being in the right place at the right time. **Jon-Erik Kello**'s big opportunity was the result of a series of phone calls back in 1989.

Vince Giordano was in need of a replacement for Randy Reinhart in the trumpet section of his Nighthawks orchestra. He heard there were a couple young horn players in the Midwest who played old style jazz. Their names were Duke Heitger and Jon-Erik Kellso.

There's a preamble to this story, so let's back up nine years. Duke was 12 years old and traveled from the family home in Toledo to Michigan to hear his father Ray play an engagement. When he heard Jon-Erik and his buddy Mike Karoub, ages 16 and 17, having a ball playing classic jazz with seasoned older players, it provided a turning point in Duke's life. On the way home, he told his Dad, "I want to do THAT," and so he has.

Getting back to 1989, Giordano made his first call to the Heitger household. Ray answered the phone. After hearing Vince's proposition, he replied, "Sorry, Duke's still in college. Besides, he's in my band. Try Jon-Erik Kellso up in Detroit," which Vince promptly did.

Giordano knew of Kellso from his work in James Dapogny's Chicago Jazz Band, so when they connected, he offered him a tryout. Jon's growing reputation had also resulted in an offer to join the Dukes of Dixieland in New Orleans to replace Frank Trapani, who had died.

"So I had two weeks of tryouts, one in New Orleans and one in New York City, and both resulted in job offers," Jon said. "It was a tough decision since I loved both cities, but I finally chose the Nighthawks because I enjoyed playing with that band and looked forward to delving into the challenging music they play. I also felt New York offered more possibilities and variety in the long run." Twenty-six years later, he is still a fixture in Giordano's 11-member aggregation.

Jon grew up in the Detroit suburb of Allen Park. When he auditioned for his elementary school band, Jon opted for the trumpet, not knowing that his father had played trumpet in swing and polka bands as a youth. So it followed that his father gave him his first lessons. He had become intrigued with his parents' collection of 78rpm Swing records, and his buddy Mike Karoub (who is a highly-regarded cellist with the Royal Garden Trio and various jazz and symphonic groups), turned him on to Bix, Louis Armstrong's Hot Five and the Eddie Condon gang as the two youngsters shared their musical discoveries.

"Dad dug out his old horn and taught me the B flat chromatic scale the first day, which might normally take weeks or even months. I was anxious to learn to play, and he got me started on the right foot before turning me over to a series of private teachers. My folks were very supportive and encouraging in my musical education. I needed no prodding, and they would often tell me to stop practicing and go to bed."

In junior high school, the two boys downsized the big swing band they had assembled in elementary school, and for two summers, they played five hours a day, six days a week outside the Henry Ford Museum in Greenfield Village at Dearborn, Michigan. "When we auditioned for the job, we knew about six tunes, so we had to learn new ones in a hurry, either by ear or from commercial arrangements that we were able to pick up. This was a great learning experience and chops-builder, and I even tried my hand at arranging and composing."

During his junior high and high school days, Jon also studied classically, playing with the International and Michigan Youth Symphonies and various community orchestras. When he was 16, he joined the musicians' union. This opened the door for him to play with older professionals, and he soon was playing with the Tailgate Ramblers and Red Garter Band.

He enrolled at Wayne State University to study music which gave him the opportunity to travel to Europe with their concert band and jazz ensembles. As his reputation grew, his work load expanded and included big bands led by Johnny Trudell and legendary drummer J.C. Heard as well as a salsa band and Motown acts that came to town.

Cornetist Tom Saunders, clarinetist Bill Roper, trumpeter Nate Panicacci and ragtime pianist Bob Milne were among those who encouraged and hired Jon and introduced him around the Detroit jazz scene. "Mike Karoub and I enjoyed going to the Presidential Inn where Saunders led his Surfside Six for many years, and he eventually let us sit in," Jon recalled. "We would sip Coca-Cola, and if we were lucky, beer out of coffee mugs trying to look like we were older. We dressed like we imagined college kids dressed – tweed or camel hair jackets with sweaters underneath, with bow ties, and Mike would sometimes smoke a cigar or pipe."

"Tommy brought Wild Bill Davison in as a guest once or twice a year, and it was a thrill listening to him share anecdotes. When I was 17, Tom included me in a 'Four Generations of Jazz Cornet" concert with himself, Wild Bill and Paul Monat. That was quite a thrill!"

"Years later, Saunders had me put a group together for the Central Illinois Jazz Festival in Decatur, and I had Mike on bass and cello, Scott Robinson on clarinet, C-melody sax and bass sax, Jeremy Kahn on piano, and Joe Ascione on drums. A very versatile group, we did everything from the Hot Five and Morton to Ellington and Ben Webster."

Moving to New York, he quickly became involved in the Nighthawks' busy schedule of regular gigs, private parties, weddings, concerts, recordings and movie soundtracks as well as becoming acquainted with the top players in town which led to more work along with being invited to jazz parties both in the States and overseas. *Chapter One*, the first recording under his own name, was with Arbors Records in 1993 and included Milt Hinton on bass. Since then, he can be heard on over 100 recordings, including six as leader.

"Playing with the Nighthawks meant that I really had to step up my game. It was total immersion, like a doctoral study of 1920s and '30s jazz. Vince's standards are very high, and the Nighthawks' book is quite demanding. I might be asked to sight-read a Red Allen solo on one tune and then do a Red Nichols solo on the next. From there, I could be expected to play in the style of a society band lead trumpet, improvise on a traditional jazz tune, fake a Latin song or a Jewish hora for the dancers– all within the same set. Vince has always been very helpful, and I've learned a ton playing with him over the years."

Since 2007, Jon has been leading the EarRegulars featuring guitarist Matt Munisteri and various guest artists on Sundays from 8 to 11 p.m. at the Ear Inn in the Soho section of Manhattan. "The building dates back to 1817 and has a warm and friendly vibe. Friends often show up after their gigs, and we pack the place. There's no cover charge, but we do have a bucket that we call Phillup DeBucket. We've had some magical nights there."

Jon-Erik can be heard on several television and movie soundtracks, including *Ghost World, The Aviator* and *Revolutionary Road* with Giordano's Nighthawks as well as the HBO series, *Broadway Empire.* the current Cinemax series, *The Knick,* and the TV movie, *Bessie,* starring Queen Latifa as Bessie Smith.

Wynton Marsalis recently asked Jon and several members of the Nighthawks to join him along with some members of his JLC band for a week-long engagement at Jazz at Lincoln Center that featured the two trumpeters in a presentation of *Louis Armstrong Continuum* honoring the Hot Five. "It was a huge honor," Jon-Erik stated.

Reflecting on his career, Jon-Erik Kellso declared, "I've surpassed all my childhood goals and had to set some new ones, which is the kind of problem you want to have. I've never had another job, and it's been everything I've ever wanted to do. As long as the phone keeps ringing, I'll just keep on doing what I've always enjoyed doing."

REBECCA KILGORE
Torchbearer for Classic Songs

Published March 2015

While she has dabbled in other genres, **Rebecca Kilgore** is a self-described torchbearer for the classic song repertoire of the Great American Songbook. She attributes her passion for preserving the vocal jazz of the 20s, 30s and 40s to the high quality of the songwriting along with heartfelt lyrics. Always putting the song ahead of the vocal, her mission over the past 30-plus years has been to learn every song from that era. "I love the old songs and in keeping the flame alive," she extols. "My goal is that when someone hears me sing, they say, 'Wow, what a beautiful song,' not 'Wow, what a great singer.'"

Becky's way with a song seems so natural that one would assume it came easily and was due to an inherent talent. But she achieved her current status as one of America's leading song stylists only partly on talent. She has paid her dues with years of hard work. She has never taken voice lessons and is essentially self-taught. "I don't do vocal exercises. I just sing. I've learned mostly from listening to other singers, and I make a point of listening to singers of different generations to absorb changes in style and delivery."

Her father majored in music at Harvard University and was a choir director. Her mother was a graphic artist. Becky did not consider herself to be especially musical growing up in Waltham, Massachusetts. "My father gave me an appreciation for music, but did not try to influence my musical tastes," she recalled. "What I heard around the house was mostly classical and choral music." When she was in high school, her father bought her a folk guitar for Christmas. She liked Joan Baez and Judy Collins and had a hazy idea of wanting to sing like them – but not in public. She would sit on the living room floor and sing her heart out when nobody was around.

Rebecca Kilgore in performance, backed by Harry Allen

She bought some sheet music, learned chords, and muddled her way along. But in the process, she discovered other music she liked when she heard Billie Holiday and Ella Fitzgerald. Suddenly, while her peers were enthralled with Elvis Presley and the Beatles, she was listening to Doris Day and Frank Sinatra.

She attended the University of Massachusetts-Amherst intending to become an artist, but after two and a half years, decided to quit college, "wanting to make my own way and be financially independent." She supported herself working a variety of jobs in the Boston area (including as a cook at the Cambridge YMCA). Still playing the guitar and singing for her own amusement, she took a few lessons, but felt she had gone as far as she could under the circumstances.

In 1979, she drove across the country to visit her sister Jenny in Portland, Oregon. She fell in love with the city and decided to stay. She got a job as a computer programmer at Reed College. But then her sister, who had moved to Portland because of a relationship, broke up with her boyfriend and moved back to Massachusetts. So

Becky was left all alone in an unfamiliar city.

A friend took her to hear some live music where she was introduced to the Wholly Cats, a 1940's swing band led by Chris Tyle. She loved the band and was captivated by the girl singer who also played guitar. Cyd Smith soon became her friend and role model. But it wasn't long before Cyd decided to move to Seattle and told Becky she should audition to take her place. After some persuasion, Becky got up her courage and got the job for what was to be the start of her professional musical career at the age of 32.

While she knew the lyrics to most of the band's songs, she underwent a crash course to learn their entire repertoire on guitar. "People occasionally ask me what's the best way to become really proficient on an instrument or with a voice," she said. "My answer is to join a band, if you can find one that will have you. You'll be pushed every second, and you have to get better to survive. It's like getting tossed into a lake and having to learn to swim or drown."

While with the Wholly Cats, she developed a love for her fellow musicians and greatly enjoyed the camaraderie. "We shared values and were committed to a common goal. We worked all the time, and it was a wonderful feeling to work so hard to achieve a shared vision." It was also Becky's first exposure to the musician's lifestyle. When the band got a six-nights-a-week gig at a recently-opened nightclub, she gave up her programming job to devote all her energies to doing what she knew was what she loved most.

After the Wholly Cats broke up in 1985, Becky freelanced with different groups, including a 13-piece band called Ranch Dressing that played in the Bob Wills tradition, and the Woody Hite Big Band. She and a friend put a country band together called Beck-a-roo that jammed on a weekly basis, and she occasionally worked with fiddle player James Mason as a duo, calling themselves Cactus Setup.

In 1992, she connected with pianist Dave Frishberg for a two-nights-a-week, five-year run at the Heathman Hotel. "Dave is one of the most respected people in the business. He made me a better singer because he plays at such a high level. Working with Dave is like having a musical conversation. No matter what kind of material I brought him, Dave would play it beautifully. How many singers are lucky enough to have an accompanist who can play anything you give him and make you sound so good doing it?"

She toured Germany with Hal Smith's California Swing Cats and was a member of Smith-led Roadrunners and Rhythm Makers quintets. She gives a lot of credit to Dan Barrett for furthering her career, a friendship that led to the formation of the Rebecca Kilgore Quartet (formerly known cvbnm as BED and including Eddie Erickson and Joel Forbes). She has been the vocalist on 50 CDs for 16 record labels. She did an interview show, On the Road with Rebecca Kilgore on radio for two years.

She has performed at jazz parties, festivals, cruises and major venues throughout the United States and Europe, including Carnegie Hall and Lincoln Center. She has been a guest on Garrison Keillor's A Prairie Home Companion and NPR's Fresh Air with Terry Gross. She was inducted into the Oregon Music Hall of Fame in 2010. She is married to Dick Titterington, a former trumpet player who has performed in Broadway shows. He doesn't mind being referred to as "Mr. Kilgore," saying "Becky is a great person. She is so modest."

Becky considers her emergence as a singer on the national stage "a minor miracle" because of her personality. "I was always shy growing up, but going on stage and performing has helped me overcome it over the years. Financially, music can be a difficult business, but I wake up every morning grateful to having a life in music. Unlike some musicians, I love to rehearse, especially new material. I'm a little like Michael Feinstein, I want to know everything about a song – who wrote it and under what circumstances, who recorded it, was it in a movie? and so forth."

Well into her 60s, Becky has no intention of slowing down. "The problem," she insists, "is that there are so many great songs. My desk is an absolute mess because of the stacks of sheet music. I'll take one off the top and incorporate it into my repertoire and then add five more to the pile. My tombstone is going to read, 'I can't go now. I haven't learned all the songs yet!'"

Legendary guitarist Bucky Pizzarelli is quoted as saying, "If Benny Goodman had a band today, Becky Kilgore would be singing with that band.

"You picked a fine time to leave me, Loose Heel..."

(Bil Keane made the notation to the right of the cartoon that he had given the original drawing to Kenny Rogers.)

TIM LAUGHLIN
New Orleans' Swinging Son

Published May 2016

Tim Laughlin [LOCK-lin] has been tabbed "The Swinging Son of New Orleans." He determined early in his career that he wanted to separate himself from other clarinet players, deciding the best way to do that was not to play higher, faster or louder, but to take a quieter, more melodic approach.

Tim favors tunes with a degree of difficulty and humor. "Tone is the biggest thing to embrace and being able to make proper use of space. It's important to tell a story, to have a lively conversation with fellow musicians fluent in a shared language."

He also opted to write original songs for the 21st century. "I began writing in the early '90s and enjoyed the results. It wasn't so much a matter of trying to change or recreate the New Orleans sound, but to have these tunes reflect how New Orleans bands played them over the past 75 years. I wanted what I composed to be representative of the city where I have lived all my life. This is a happy, joyful place. New Orleans is a state of mind. We're not in a big hurry, and we love people. The music reflects that. It's about the ensemble, dance music, and movement."

One of the dozen or so CDs Tim has recorded is *The Isle of Orleans* that was released in 2003. He was the first New Orleans clarinetist to produce an album of all original tunes, backed by a band that included Connie Jones, Hal Smith, Lucien Barbarin, Jason Marsalis, Tom McDermott, John Royen, and Matt Perrine, among others. Some of his songs are included in the credits of numerous films and television shows.

Tom McDermott's liner notes captured the moment: "If you live in New Orleans and make your living playing traditional jazz, you have some choices as to what music you're going to play. You can cave in completely to tourist demand and blare out nothing but the Dixieland Top 40, then complain about how little you're working. Or you can excavate the mustiest regions of the repertoire, perform neglected works by the 1923 "Hog Jowls" Jackson band, brag that nobody else ever plays that stuff, then complain about how little you're working.

"With 20 years' experience in the music wars, Tim Laughlin has done some of both. Fortunately, he started writing and performing his own tunes. Tim came to the conclusion that 'If I'm going to play obscure music, it might as well be my own.'" McDermott concluded, "For if music like traditional jazz is to survive, it not only needs fresh performers and audiences, but new melodies to keep things from getting stale."

Tim fell in love with the sound of the clarinet when he heard a young friend in his neighborhood play the instrument. He got his first horn at 9 (which now is a lamp in his home). His first teacher, Bill Bourgeois, was a childhood friend of Irving Fazola and Eddie Miller, and played in Sharkey Bonano's band and with Leon Prima. Tim's first job was playing on a Mardi Gras float with high school classmates at 15.

When he was 17, he met Pete Fountain and eventually became a member of the clarinet icon's Half-Fast Walking Club band, a popular krewe on Mardi Gras day. In 2009, following the Roosevelt Hotel's post-Katrina restoration, the two headlined the reopening of the legendary Blue Room before sold-out crowds. When Tim and his wife had a private audience with Pope Francis at the Vatican, Tim was carrying "Ole Betsy," the horn Fountain played in his early career. "We received a Papal blessing along with anything we were carrying with us at the time."

When Hurricane Katrina hit the Gulf Coast, Tim and his bandmates were about to leave for a festival in South America, forcing them to drive all night to stay ahead of the storm and make their flight. After Katrina, the U.S. State Department sent Tim on a goodwill tour of Peru, Mexico and Canada as a thank-you gesture for giving aid to the Gulf Coast. A concert in Merida, Mexico, raised $30,000 for the New Orleans Center for the Creative Arts to help replace lost instruments.

Besides Fountain, others who have had an influence on his playing include Kenny Davern, Jack Maheu and Bob Wilber, all melodic players. His mentor Connie Jones, with whom Tim played innumerable times over the past 20 years, taught him how to lead a band, the use of space and phrasing, and how to find the platinum notes. Keep it loose was the veteran cornetist's advice. Pete invited Connie and Tim to join his band at Hollywood Casino in Bay St. Louis from 2009-2012. Tim also played and toured with the DUKES of Dixieland for four years (1989-93).

One of Tim's house concerts with legendary pianist Dick Hyman

On the personal side, Tim and his wife Juliet enjoy hosting house concerts with friends and visitors at their home in keeping with the New Orleans tradition of "the salon." Guest artists at these sold-out concerts have included Dick Hyman, Wendell Brunious, Don Vappie and Evan Christopher. (Tim has written a handbook on how to host a house party.)

Before meeting his future wife in 2006 Tim was a committed renter and had spent years renting in the French Quarter, enjoying the flexibility and low maintenance. Juliet, who is an investor and owner of commercial properties, convinced him on the merits of ownership, and in 2008 they found a sprawling building for sale in the 800 block of Royal Street.

It was a classic Creole, three-story main house built in 1811, with a carriage house and courtyard at the rear. But extensive renovations were required, and workmen worked throughout the summer and fall so that by early December the house was ready to serve as the site of the couple's wedding. The property currently is not just a home but a place of business with an art gallery fronting Royal Street, along with multiple rental apartments and parking spaces. The couple live on the second floor which features a spacious ballroom where concerts and rehearsals are held.

Tim has found his niche as a staple of the Crescent City music scene where on any night he may be holding forth playing his favorite instrument at the Palm Court Jazz Cafe, Bombay Club Martini Bar, Snug Harbor or on the Steamboat Natchez. He sums it all up by saying, "My biggest delight is knowing I am continuing a great tradition of keeping a timeless art form alive, and making a living at it."

DAN LEVINSON
"Having a Great Time Playing Jazz"
Published October 2014

Dan Levinson attributes whatever success he has achieved in his 26 years as a professional musician to the mentoring he received from two veterans who took the time to further his career. He says the late Rosy McHargue taught him most of what he knows about music and life. From a six-year association with pianist Dick Hyman, he learned the business side of the profession. Today he is filling that mentoring role for many up-and-coming musicians who have sought him out seeking advice and direction.

Growing up in the Los Angeles area, Dan studied piano and guitar, but says, "I really didn't have the discipline to learn them." In his early teens, he discovered early jazz listening to records borrowed from the Santa Monica Public Library. One was a 1950 RCA recording of *The Best of Dixieland*, and the tune that really got his attention was *Livery Stable Blues* by the Original Dixieland Jazz Band.

That prompted him to return to the piano to learn ragtime, but he acknowledged he couldn't read music very well. He took trumpet and clarinet lessons and settled on the latter, which he considered the easier of the two instruments. But his interest was primarily in the theater, and he became at drama major at New York University.

On a visit home, his father suggested they go hear 82-year-old saxophonist Rosy McHargue who was leading a band at a Santa Monica steakhouse. To 19-year-old Dan, Rosy was a celebrity who had been around when jazz was in its infancy. Rosy had met Bix Beiderbecke, knew Benny Goodman, recorded with Frankie Trambauer, and been a member of the Ted Weems and Kay Kyser big bands.

"Rosy didn't treat me the way I see some musicians treating people

108

in the audience, giving them an impersonal greeting and quickly moving on. Rosy invited me to his apartment to listen to records. Later on, he tried to talk me out of being a musician, but everything he said was encouraging. He wasn't optimistic about the state of the music, saying, 'In the old days, if you played your instrument well, you could make a living, but it's not that way now.' Well, I found a niche, and I'm making a living."

Back in New York City, he practiced the clarinet constantly and visited all the clubs that featured traditional jazz. Along the way, he struck up a friendship with ragtime pianist Max Morath. Shortly before Dan was due to graduate from NYU, Max told him that Dick Hyman was looking for an assistant to catalogue Dick's huge record and tape collection, file correspondence and run errands.

Dan took what appeared to be a fairly routine job, but said, "Because Dick was away much of the time, my function became much more significant. I was the one who held down the fort, mailing out publicity material, filling record orders and even copying music. Dick is a great businessman, and if there was a problem, he always came up with a solution. He was especially good at dealing with other musicians."

This association continued for six years, interrupted by a year traveling through 17 countries in Europe, six months in New Orleans, and tours with Leon Redbone. Dick also counseled Dan that he should learn to play the saxophone. "Reluctantly, I got an alto sax and took lessons. A year later, I got my hands on a C-melody sax, and now I play all the saxophones from soprano down to baritone."

"I gave up any thoughts about pursuing a career in the theater, not wanting to end up as a waiter in some New York restaurant, which happens to many aspiring actors. But from the start, I was fortunate that I was working constantly as a musician. I was young and enthusiastic - the new kid on the block – and that seem to appeal to people."

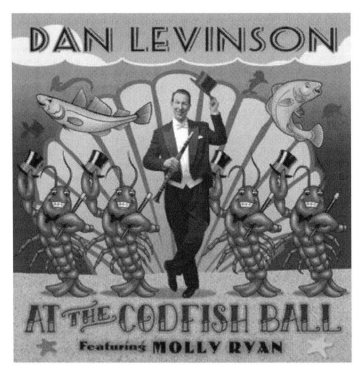

Dan is one of the most prolific reedmen on the jazz circuit, both as a leader and sideman, and his busy schedule takes him around the world to perform. His tributes to Benny Goodman have brought him many accolades over the years. His own ensembles vary considerably in style and repertoire, running the gamut from ragtime to early jazz and swing. He has performed on over 150 CDs, including nine under his own name, and a prominent Dutch discographer has even published a separate booklet on Dan's many recordings as part of his *Swinging Americans* series.

Dan knows from experience it is important to encourage young musicians. One night at Eddie Condon's club 30 years ago, he met trombonist Dan Barrett who offered to share his extensive record collection with the then-19-year-old clarinetist and also got him to do some arranging. Banjoist Eddy Davis is another who promoted Dan, often inviting him to sit in with his band.. Dan is currently living in Eddy's old apartment on Washington Square in the Big Apple, which is directly above the apartment once occupied by Eddie Condon.

As he approaches his 50th birthday, Dan gets great satisfaction in reaching out to young musicians to share his knowledge and experience as a jazz musician. "I don't see helping a younger person as a threat to my livelihood. They are the future of this music. Many don't take the time to research the history and tradition of the music, and they no longer have direct links to the people whose music they play. But when they are exposed, their minds are like sponges."

Certainly a prime beneficiary of Dan's largesse is vocalist Molly Ryan. The two met at the Sacramento Jubilee, and Dan admits it was love at first sight. He had been battling throat cancer which compromised his ability to speak. "I no longer sing because I've been married to my favorite singer since 2008. She's my voice," the always-dapper Dan Levinson said with a smile.

(The Levinson family now includes daughter Aven, born in 2017.)

JIM MARTINEZ
Many Talents, Many Roles

Published August 2018

Jim Martinez is a man of many talents who wears many hats. He is a versatile pianist and organist, a Steinway artist, recording artist, concert promoter, teacher, businessman, graphic/web designer, worship leader and minister of music.

The California native began his musical career at the age of four, received 18 years of classical training, and has since amassed a list of musical accomplishments encompassing nearly all styles of music.

The plan was to become a classical pianist, but it was in his junior year that his high school jazz band needed a piano player, and he was hooked. Getting established in his career barely in his early 20s, he found that he could stay busy by booking his own concerts rather than waiting for the phone to ring for an engagement. He's been doing it for the past 20 years.

Looking to getting involved in the annual Sacramento Traditional Jazz Festival, he offered to play gratis in the lobby of the host hotel. The Festival director made note of the large crowds he attracted, and Jim was a regular performer over the next 15 years. When Big Tiny Little suddenly passed away prior to appearing at the Dixieland Monterey Festival, Jim was called to replace him, which meant brushing up on his ragtime, Dixieland and swing repertoire.

He performed, toured and recorded with an impressive list of jazz notables. He's been booked at Yoshi's San Francisco and the Basemen Jazz Club in Sydney, Australia. For 13 straight years, he opened All-Star Night at the Lionel Hampton Jazz Festival in Moscow, Idaho. He gained international exposure through his *Echoes of Oscar Peterson* concerts in Denmark.

He's become associated with the music the late Vince Guaraldi who wrote and performed his original tunes for the *Peanuts* television series. Jim's quartet has been presenting *A Charlie Brown Christmas* holiday concerts from California to Florida over the past 20 years. His most recent project, *Good Grief! It's Still Jim Martinez - A Tribute to Vince Guaraldi, Charles Schulz & Peanuts* peaked at #10 on the national RMR Jazz charts and was on the *Jazz Week* charts a total of 26 weeks.

Ever the promoter, Jim saw an opportunity to fill a musical void with the demise of the Sacramento Music & Jazz Festival after holding forth over the Memorial Day weekend for 44 years. In just five months, he organized, promoted and held a one-day festival with 31 bands in Roseville, a suburban community 20 miles northeast of Sacramento. He projected 500 attendees as his breakeven; the event drew 1,000. Asked to assess his success in so many areas, Jim Martinez responds: "A lot of hard work and prayer."

THE MEIJERS
Cruising to Jazz

Published August 2016

When Alida and Pieter Meijers first came to the United States from The Netherlands in 1968, they expected to stay only a year while Pieter completed his post-doctoral appointment at the Brookhaven National Laboratory on Long Island. A year later, they were in Cairo, Egypt where Pieter taught a course in archeological chemistry at the American University. It was back to New York in 1970 where for the next decade, Pieter would work as a research chemist at the Brookhaven Lab and Metropolitan Museum of Art and organized a Dixieland jazz band, the Isotope Stompers.

Alida kept busy while Pieter was immersed in his work and in 1973, was approached by a friend who had just opened a travel agency, suggesting she might enjoy the travel field because of her extensive travel experience and proficiency in foreign languages. "I knew nothing about the travel industry, but agreed to give it a try for a week at no pay," she recalled. "I loved it! Clients would come in to book a trip to Italy, for example, and were told 'Alida has been to

Italy. Why don't you talk to her.'"

She went on to work as a travel consultant at several offices and obtained her Certified Travel Consultant diploma (CTC) in 1984. The idea of combining travel and jazz was always in the back of her mind, so that year she took two bands –the California Nightblooming Jazzmen and Desert City 6 from Phoenix – to Holland for a concert tour with 80 fans joining them. The highlight of the trip was a festival at Eindoven called Jazzdagen ("Jazz Days" in Dutch), which became the name of her company.

She deals with several cruise lines, including Holland America, Crystal and Regent Seven Seas and also charters river boats. She books an average of six cruises and tours a year, which she always accompanies with a staff member. She hires bands and musicians who have a following and "those who need to be heard - like Fat Babies from Chicago" and pays the musicians a per diem fee comparable to what they receive for a weekend festival (plus expenses). The musicians' spouses can come along by paying for their airline tickets and a small surcharge. Saying she gets her satisfaction when everyone has a great time, she emphasizes that she has never had to cancel a cruise because of not meeting the contracted minimum reservations.

Alida grew up in a small town near Amersfoort in Central Netherlands. She took up guitar at age 9 and accompanied herself singing pop songs in different languages. Although she sang in several musical productions, she says, "I've always sung, but I'm not really a singer." She met Pieter in 1962 during a College Spring Break and remembered how they would perform on the beach during the day hoping they would be hired by a local restaurant or bar in the evening. The couple were married in 1965.

She learned to play the rhythm guitar and tenor banjo, and for the next 25 years, played, sang and recorded with various bands, retiring as a performer in 1997 to devote more time to her growing business.

The Meijers moved to Los Angeles in 1981 when Pieter was hired by the Los Angeles County Museum of Art as Senior Research Chemist and later Head of Conservation specializing in the nuclear study of works of art. He retired in 2000, but still has an office at the Museum. Both Meijers, who are avid opera fans, played with the Nightblooming Jazzman, and since 1998, Pieter has been the leader of the High Sierra Jazz Band.

At age 6, Pieter played in a concert band that his father conducted in the coastal community of Oostkapelle, and he did some conducting of classical orchestras himself in his mid 20's. He identifies Jan Morks, a fellow countryman and clarinetist best known for his work with the Dutch Swing College Band, as his biggest jazz influence. Academically, he has doctoral degrees in radiochemistry and nuclear physics from the University of Amsterdam. Always active in sports, he was a champion swimmer and played footbol (soccer) and tennis until he was 40 and as with most Weekend Warriors, is now dealing with back and knee issues.

His impressive resume shows he is the author or co-author of several book, has written scholarly articles for more than 50 publications, is a Fellow and past president of the American Institute for Conservation of Historic and Artistic Works, and for five years was associate editor of *Archaeometry,* a publication that deals with the dating of materials and the relationship of the physical and biological sciences pertaining to archaeology and art history.

Having arranged more than 300 cruises and tours and circumnavigated the globe several times over with talented jazz musicians and enthusiastic jazz lovers over the past 32 years, Alida Meijers has had great success in promoting the idea that "Jazzdagen Tours harmonizes the love of music and the love of travel with such meticulous orchestration that those who have enjoyed one of their cruises or tours are unable to enjoy one without the other."

MIDIRI BROTHERS
Exciting Small Group Swing

Published November 2013

While they may make occasional references to the fact that they are twins as part of the casual banter they carry on between numbers on the bandstand, **Joe and Paul Midiri** prefer not to make a big deal of the fact that Paul is one minute older than his brother. They would rather that people recognize and remember them for their authentic and highly creative performances of the music associated with Benny Goodman, Artie Shaw, Lionel Hampton, Red Norvo and the Dorsey Brothers, whether it be part of a trio, quintet, sextet or 16-piece big band.

One critic wrote, "I've seen and heard hundreds of clarinet players, but Joe Midiri is the best. I'm enthralled by his tone, technique, creativity, imagination and sound along with some Louis Armstrong scat singing." Lionel Hampton was the inspiration for Paul in doubling on the vibraphone and drums. His multi-instrument talents, which also include the trombone, lend a special versatility to the Midiri band's unique sound and diverse arrangements.

When asked about their musical philosophy, the response was, "Music is a language where you are speaking to people. It's constantly evolving. It's all about communications. Music relaxes the audience, and they therefore enjoy it more. We love what we are doing and feel blessed." Quoting a saying attributed to comedian Red Skelton, they added, "What we are is God's gift to us; what we become is our gift to God."

The Midiri brothers had an auspicious beginning of life. Their mother had lost twin girls before the two boys were born. When she again became pregnant, her pediatrician determined that she would deliver just one baby. It wasn't until the actual delivery by Cesarean section on June 3, 1958 that it became apparent that two baby boys were about to come into the world – a minute apart.

The family lived in Runnemede, New Jersey, just across the Delaware River from Philadelphia where the father worked in the Navy Yard. Growing up, the young Midiris' interests were in history, trains, gardening and soccer. It wasn't until they were 16 that music became part of their lives when they were recruited by high school chums to join the school band. What really sold Joe, who thought he wanted to become a lawyer, was hearing a Benny Goodman radio concert from the London Palladium on New Year's Eve.

The duo went on to Glassboro State College (now Rowan University) where Joe majored in music and Paul in history, graduating in 1983. They formed a Dixieland band that took part in the Southern Comfort collegiate competition and honed their skills playing with older musicians who proved to be great mentors.

While in college, Joe suffered nerve damage that required surgery, and his hand atrophied. He used a tennis ball to regain strength, but his recovery was not progressing to his satisfaction. One day when he was in the college library, he overheard an instructor tell a student off in no uncertain terms. He decided he needed a highly disciplined approach and engaged the hard-driving teacher who proceeded to put him through some difficult drills that ultimately led to complete recovery. "It was like learning to play all over again," he recalled.

In 1992, Paul at the age of 34 was doing substitute teaching, playing drums in the band and working in a music store. One day a customer brought a vibraphone into the store and said he would sell it for $25. Paul figured that was too good a deal to pass up and after consulting with the store manager, took the $25 out of his next pay check. The vibes became Paul's primary instrument, and Jimmy Lawler, who had been the band's vocalist, took over the drummer's seat.

The Midiris built quite a following over the years working up and down the East Coast, with occasional ventures as far west as Chicago. They were featured for a time on the New Orleans Bandstand at the Showboat Casino in Atlantic City where they would occasionally play free concerts in the lobby. There's a story that the brothers would sometimes split up, with one working the front lobby, the other out on the promenade. One day a well-oiled patron who was departing the premises ran into Joe on the promenade and asked, "How did you get here so fast? And what happened to your trombone?"

New Jersey concert promoter Bruce Gast is credited with helping the Midiris line up their first festival engagement in 2001 in Connecticut. Members of the Titan Hot 5 heard them and passed favorable comments along to other festival directors, as did the late Bob Finch. With typical depreciating humor, Finch told the Orange County hierarchy that "the band is really mediocre," but that didn't deter John Dieball from hiring them for their first West Coast engagement in 2002.

A call soon followed from Ken Coulter who said, "I never hire a band without personally hearing them, but I'm going to make an exception because Bob Finch said I've got to hire you," resulting in their first of many appearances at the annual Mammoth Jazz Festival in 2003. Mammoth has become one of the Midiris' favorites except for the year it took two days and 13 hours of travel time because of delayed and cancelled flights for the band to travel cross-country.

Evidence of the compatibility that exists between the two brothers, Paul acknowledges "We have a relationship where the younger brother is the boss of the older brother and the better musician, I might add." L.A. Jazz Magazine advised its readers "to catch them whenever you can. Their sextet is one of the most exciting small group swing units around today." So the Midiris continue to make great music while having to tolerate all the bad twin jokes, like the one about why the Siamese twins moved to London."

Answer: "So the other one could drive."

THE FAMILY CIRCUS.   By Bil Keane

"I'll be the starter. On your mark . . . Ready
. . . Get set . . ."

BUTCH MILES
Setting the Standard

Published October 2015

Through decades of playing with the biggest names in jazz and popular music, **Charles "Butch" Miles** has earned the reputation as one of the country's most dynamic drummers. While described by some as "flamboyant and flashy," he more appropriately is known for great technique, precision timing, creative finesse, youthful imagination and unending energy. "Low passion is not my style," he states.

He has played and recorded with everyone from Frank Sinatra, Lena Horne and Ella Fitzgerald to Benny Goodman, Tony Bennett and

Itzak Pearlman. He has performed at all the major jazz festival throughout the world, recorded 130 albums (including four GRAMMY winners), and appeared in three movies and on the major television talk shows hosted by Johnny Carson, Merv Griffin, Dick Cavett, Mike Douglas, Jerry Lewis Telethon, plus *60 Minutes*. In 1976 while with the Basie band, he played a Royal Command Performance for Her Majesty the Queen of England which was televised throughout Europe. In 2011, he was inducted into the West Virginia Music Hall of Fame and has been honored on the floors of the West Virginia and Texas state senates.

Several of his drumming peers say it best. Hal Smith comments, "Butch Miles' great drumming demonstrates his respect for the swing tradition of giants such as Buddy Rich, Gene Krupa and Papa Jo Jones, whom he considers his favorites. But Butch always looks forward -- not back. He has a wonderful time-feel, a gift for improvisation, fantastic technique, superb musical taste...and the ability to swing no matter what!"

Ed Metz Jr., remembers, "I took lessons from Butch when I was 12 years old. He taught me the right techniques and showed me examples of how different drummers play along with a few tricks of the trade. He stressed that a drummer can't slack off and has to be consistent throughout an entire number and give a 100%, all-out performance every night. He obviously has had a huge influence on my career."

Danny Coots joins in, "Butch Miles is a joyous player from whom I still learn. He has phenomenal technique and a great understanding of the music and what his function is. Always tasteful and visually exciting, he is the consummate drummer who can bring out the best in any band."

Butch Miles began playing the snare drum at the age of 9, got his first drum set at 14, and a year later was being tutored by veteran drummer Frank Thompson. Honing his skill at local clubs in Charleston, West Virginia where out-of-town musicians gathered, he soon joined the Musicians Union and was playing in local dance bands. He went on to major in music at West Virginia State University (1962-66), and after graduating, toured the Eastern United States with the Iris Bell Trio for a year.

He next moved to Ann Arbor, Michigan where a two-year engagement at a popular supper club turned into a seven-year stay along with teaching at a local music store. His first big break was with Mel Torme in 1971. In 1975, he was temporarily out of work and was thinking about becoming a court reporter. But a fortuitous call from Sonny Cohn, road manager for the Count Basie Orchestra, saying that Ray Parello, the band's drummer, was injured in an automobile accident and asking if Butch would fill in for a few days.

Described as "the perfect Basie drummer," he obviously has many stories to relate about his years with Basie. "I'd been with the band just a short while, and Basie hadn't said anything about my playing," he recalled. "I mentioned it to Cohn, who just smiled and said, "Don't worry. If something is wrong, Basie will tell you."

"Longtime band guitarist Freddie Green was the epitome of time-keeping, and I relied on him to stay on track. I could also see Basie's foot next to the piano pedal, which also helped me determine the right tempo." As to why he left the Basie band in 1979, he said, "As great as it was night-after-night playing *April in Paris, Shiny Stockings* and *Corner Pocket,* I just wanted something different." He joined the Dave Brubeck Quartet for a year, saying, "I had a ball playing with both groups."

After leading the Jazz Express for 15 years, Butch returned to the Basie band in 1997 for another 10 years. Assessing the Basie style,

Butch said, "Bill Basie described his music as 'pat-yer-foot,' meaning that if the music gets to you, the beat gets to you, the whole thing begins to give you something you can relate and react to, then tap your foot, pat in time, snap your fingers, tilt your head, hit your knee, and get up and dance."

For the past eight years, he has been a professor in the School of Music at Texas State University-San Marcos. He conducts clinics at colleges and high schools and tells aspiring drummers that listening is the key, although acknowledging he would like to change the attitude of some young drummers.

In 2014, he found he had difficulty breathing and was diagnosed with idiopathic pulmonary fibrosis for which there is no treatment other than a lung transplant. It's a disease where tissue deep in the lungs becomes thick and stiff over time. As the tissue thickens, the lungs cannot properly move oxygen into the bloodstream, resulting in the brain and other organs not getting the oxygen they need.

He underwent a lung transplant, the recovery has gone well, and he was back on the bandstand seven months after the transplant. He did report that he has had to change his drumming style slightly because of fatigue in his left arm when playing due to the steroids he has been taking.

About living in Texas where he is a past president of the Austin Jazz Society, he states "The thing about living in Texas is that musicians here encompass a huge spectrum of music. They don't just play one style, and the music always swings."

And so the beat goes on.

KEN PEPLOWSKI
Super Clarinet

Published June 2017

It was a jazz critic from Great Britain writing for the BBC in 2013 who anointed Ken Peplowski with super star status when he declared that the versatile clarinetist from Garfield Heights, Ohio is "arguably the greatest living jazz clarinetist." He was the 2014 recipient of Sarasota Jazz Festival's "Satchmo Award" given for his "unique and enduring contributions to the living history of jazz," and he's been inducted into the Jazz Cruise Hall of Fame.

Ken Peplowski with Brazilian guitarist Diego Figueriedo

He's been touted as a worthy successor to Benny Goodman, especially in terms of similar tone and virtuosity, and the fact that both are considered "crossover" musicians who seriously perform classical music in addition to jazz. The comparison has also been made that Peplowski sounds the way Goodman might sound today if the legendary King of Swing had continued to polish his craft and expand his musical purview into the 21st Century.

Ken has great respect for Goodman, calling him "one of the greatest clarinetists of all time, as well as an outstanding bandleader whose bands will always rank among the very best in the annals of jazz. Benny was such a giant figure that he is almost unparalleled."

Ken Peplowski came from a family where there was always music in the house. His father was an amateur musician who played the accordion, and his older brother Ted took up the trumpet. The three family members were in a Polish polka band, the Harmony Kings, where Ken said he learned his craft "by doing it. When you grow up in Cleveland and play in a Polish polka band, you learn to think on your feet in a hurry."

After his first public appearance, he recalled, "I knew this is what I wanted to do, and I enjoyed actually making money at that early age." By the time he was in high school, he was writing music for an assigned project and playing in the school stage band, teaching at the local music store, and playing jazz gigs around town while still getting up early every morning for school. "It let me be creative, and it's where I learned to improvise and about chord changes, and how to 'fake' songs. It was like learning to swim by getting thrown in the water."

He went on to attend Cleveland State University as a music major where the curriculum emphasis was on classical music. To keep his jazz chops, Ken would sneak off to play with local jazz bands on weekends to help pay for his tuition.

In the late 70s, Ken had a quartet and was playing at a Cleveland jazz festival where he was heard by Buddy Morrow, leader of the Tommy Dorsey Orchestra, who made him an offer on the spot to join the band to not only play lead alto, but also have a featured number on clarinet with the rhythm section. He was with the band for two and a half years, describing the experience as "a great road-school playing one-nighters 48 weeks out of the year."

While on the road with the Dorsey band, Ken met the late saxophonist Sonny Stitt and had the opportunity to study with him. "He was an inspiration to all of us who make a living performing on the road. I've never heard anyone play with such amazing consistency as Sonny in all kinds of settings."

After a short tour with the road company of the Broadway show, *Annie*, Ken moved to New York City in 1980 and was soon playing everything from Dixieland to avant-garde jazz. "Playing all those weddings and private parties and working at jazz clubs like Condon's was a terrific experience, because you learn to deal with the unpredictable."

In the mid-80s, Benny Goodman came out of retirement to lead what was to be his last band. It included Ken and such stalwarts as Bucky Pizzarelli, Dick Hyman and Flip Phillips. Goodman was known for his impatience with musicians who didn't perform up to his standards and would often fire those who hit the wrong notes on the spur of the moment. (Some did get rehired, however, when Benny cooled down.) Ken, who had become the band's unofficial "straw boss," was one of two band members who wasn't unceremoniously ushered off the bandstand.

Although that band was together for only about a year and played limited engagements, the experience had a significant impact on Peplowski. *(He shared some of his thoughts regarding Benny Goodman in a 2013 interview with Jesse Cloninger, when both were involved with the Oregon Festival of American Music.)*

Currently on the road roughly half the year, Ken has played

everything from small clubs to the Hollywood Bowl for a sold-out concert. He's been on the stage of Radio City Music Hall sharing the billing with Frank Sinatra and Ella Fitzgerald. He's headlined in Las Vegas, the Newport Jazz Festival, pops concerts and European festivals and been on soundtracks for Woody Allen films.

His versatility was on display at the Siletz Bay Music Festival in Lincoln City, Oregon when he participated in two weeks of jazz and classical music performances and community outreach programs. He performed German composer Max Bruch's "Double Concerto for Clarinet and Viola, op. 88, mov. 1" and Brahm's "Trio in A Minor, op.11x" along with a Benny Goodman medley and a tribute to Leonard Bernstein, plus hosting "An Evening of Comedy and Music" with comedian Pete Barbutti.

He enjoys doing intimate house parties, of which he does about 10 a year, mainly in New York and California. "These are mainly 'add-on' engagements to an existing tour or concert commitment. The host will put me with a group of musicians of his choice, which gets me playing all kinds of different music. We don't rehearse, and it all usually happens in somebody's living room. So we're creating something right in front of the audience, after which we have an open forum. It's a fun evening and provides those in attendance with a look inside of what we do as musicians when we collaborate with other people."

Known for his humorous outlook, he admits, "I love being on stage, but I sometimes get bored. That's when the jokes come in handy. It's not a crime to show that you enjoy what you are doing." When he's a sideman on another musician's gig, he is always the total professional and makes no effort to upstage the lead artist.

Ken has recorded some 50 CDs as a soloist and been a sideman on over 400 with other artists. He says he's most proud of his recordings because "They capture what I do and hopefully have made an impact on people." He recorded a Big Band CD for Arbors Records and has even done a couple CDs that sell with *Menus & Music* interactive cookbooks.

Always willing to give back to his profession, Peplowski does workshops for students of all ages and abilities. "My goal is to get students to learn how to teach themselves and how to bring out their own best qualities. After all, jazz is about individuality. First, you learn the rules, and then you figure out how to break them. I like to think of myself as a lifelong student." The advice he gives to aspiring young musicians is "You must have a burning desire to succeed more than anything in your life."

Asked what's ahead, he responds, "Who knows. I love all kinds of music, and I'd like to find more opportunities to bridge the gaps between different musical styles. I consider myself an interpreter of material. If something interests me, I try to put my own spin on it without thinking or worrying about playing a particular style. Basically, I like a challenge. I'm a sucker for a good melody, and I love playing for audiences, big or small."

CHUCK REDD
A Drummer's Odyssey

Published December 2017

Chuck Redd has a growing reputation as one of the top performers on the jazz circuit today who is equally adept on the drums and vibraphone, and who had the good fortune to have been influenced, mentored and to have performed with some of the true masters of his craft.

His parents were not musicians, but loved music, so Chuck and his brother heard a lot of music around the house. "Growing up in the '60s, I always associated music with joy and fun, and after hearing Gene Krupa and Buddy Rich, there wasn't any question that I wanted to play the drums. I took lessons on the snare drum at age 10, played in school bands, and began to dabble on the vibes while in high school."

It was while attending Montgomery Community College that he came under the tutelage of pianist/composer/arranger Bill Potts. "Bill really taught me about music, and he took me on my first trip to New

York City to hear some real jazz. I sat in with Al Cohn at the 1976 Manassas Jazz Festival when I was 18 as the youngest musician in that year's lineup."

Chuck free-lanced around the Washington, DC metro area, taking advantage of any and all opportunities to gain experience. His first big break came when he was 21, and he began touring the globe as one-third of the Charlie Byrd Trio. That led to joining up with the Great Guitars, a group that included Byrd, Barney Kessel and Herb Ellis. For five years, he was the featured vibraphonist with the Mel Torme All-Star Quintet, which included two concerts at Carnegie Hall.

He has made over 25 European tours and six tours of Japan with artists such as Ken Peplowski, Terry Gibbs, Conte Candoli, and the Benny Goodman Tribute Orchestra. He performed at the White House with the Barney Kessel Trio, has appeared on The Tonight Show, and traveled to Africa with the Dizzy Gillespie Quintet to celebrate the Namibian Independence.

Gunther Schuller hired Redd to become a member of the Smithsonian Jazz Masterworks Orchestra, an assignment that lasted for 15 years. Chuck served as artist-in-residence at the Smithsonian Jazz Café (2004-2008) and was the featured soloist in the finale concert at the Lionel Hampton International Jazz Festival with the Lionel Hampton Big Band and the Clayton-Hamilton Jazz Orchestra. He calls a 2007 appearance with the Milt Jackson Tribute Band "one of my greatest honors."

Chuck acknowledges that he was profoundly influenced by drummers like Jake Hanna, Shelly Manne, Grady Tate and Mel Lewis who, in his words, "had exquisite taste and technique and kept great time. Jake Hanna told me 'Taste is something you learn.' The music comes first; the drumming is second. It is important to respect the melody and have the ability to swing."

His recording of *When Redd is Blue,* that included his younger brother Robert, who is an established pianist in the D.C. area and a member of the Duke Ellington Orchestra and the Wolf Trap Jazz Trio, is just one of 80 recordings that feature Chuck's musical talents. He can also be heard on the soundtracks of *The Great Chefs* television series and the NPR broadcast of *Jazz Smithsonian.*

While teaching at the University of Maryland School of Music, Chuck still maintains a busy performing schedule (mainly in the New York City metropolitan area where he has worked extensively with most of the well-known New York-based musicians) and traveling about the country for jazz parties and festivals and at concert venues. He was the 2014 honoree at the Roswell (NM) Jazz Festival and winner of the *Hot House Jazz Magazine* Fan-Decision Award as the best vibraphonist in 2015 and 2016.

Asked what advice he gives his students, he tells them, "I believe the best approach is to identify the music and musicians that move you, do your best to imitate them, and then move deeper to a level where you play your own way. The greatest artists have always done this."

In stating his view of jazz today, he observed, "The outlook is mixed, but I stay optimistic. There are certainly more concerts now, which hopefully means we are reaching a bigger audience. However, that setting can be less intimate than a club. Either way, we want people to smile, tap their toes and be moved. Musicians can achieve this as long as they are playing with sincerity and passion."

The promo for a recent appearance at Dizzy's Club Coca Cola at Jazz at Lincoln Center summed up Chuck's career very succinctly, stating: "There are two things you can always count on when Chuck Redd is performing: a top-notch band, and swinging takes on timeless standards in the jazz, blues and American popular song idioms."

REYNOLDS BROTHERS
Grandsons of Famed Movie Star

Published January 2015

"She was like the Easter Bunny and Santa Claus rolled into one, just the best grandmother ever. It was fun to be with her."

This is the way **Ralf and John Reynolds** remember their maternal grandmother, movie star ZaSu Pitts who appeared in over 500 silent dramas and comedies and later comedy sound films; traded banter on the radio with Bing Crosby, Al Jolson and Rudy Vallee; and numbered Walt Disney, Richard Nixon and Ronald Reagan among her friends. Her first substantive film (at age 23) was *The Little Princess* starring Mary Pickford in 1917. Her last role was as a switchboard operator in the madcap Stanley Kramer comedy, *It's a Mad, Mad, Mad, Mad World* in 1963. She was honored on a U.S. postage stamp in 1994 along with nine other stars of the silent screen.

Her unusual name (pronounced "say-zoo") derived from a combination of the names of her father's sisters, Eliza and Susan, to satisfy competing family interests. The boys' mother was named ZaSu Ann, but went by Ann. Ralf has a picture of his grandmother introducing him to Vice President Nixon at the dedication of the Matterhorn at Disneyland on opening day in 1959. They also recall going to the studio when she was filming episodes of *The Gale Storm Show*.

Growing up in Pasadena, Ralf remembers his grandfather played the bones to the accompaniment of records by the Lu Watters, Turk Murphy and Firehouse 5 + 2 bands. Ralf's musical career started in junior high school when he heard Glenn Miller's *In the Mood* that led to taking up the saxophone, clarinet and flute. He switched to bass instruments while attending the University of Oregon School of Music and has been known to play the sousaphone, piccolo, guitar, string bass and drums on occasion. He was a member of the All-American College Band at Disney World in 1974.

He has degrees in history and social science from Biola University and over time spent a decade as a high school teacher in Newport Beach and San Juan Capistrano. At the age of 22 while playing for the cocktail hour at Rosie O'Grady's in a trio along with Jim Mahack and Randy Morris, it was suggested he learn to play the washboard. He purchased a washboard and attached the strap from his guitar. While his initial audition did not go well, by trial-and-error, he soon became a proficient "washboarder".

Ralf had aspirations to be an Army officer, but instead became a Calvary scout assigned to Fort Carson in Colorado where Major General Colin Powell was in charge. By 1989, he was working at Pleasure Island in Florida and later at the Magic Kingdom at Disney World. Back in California, he managed a thrift store for a church, and in 2011 the Rhythm Rascals became a contract band at the Disney California Adventure theme park in Anaheim where they perform three days a week.

Ralf has designed the washboards he uses and are custom-made of stainless steel for fast action and long wear. He says a regular washboard would wear out in a month. He used to have a double-sided washboard which swung open to reveal an "Applause" sign opposite a picture of Betty Boop, but discontinued using it when the added thickness of the board caused aggravated tendonitis by his constant playing.

John, who is two years younger than Ralf, picked up the 5-string banjo at age 10 and then taught himself to play the 4-string. While attending Monterey Peninsula College, he played in a band with Herb Miller, Glenn's brother. The band used a number of hand-written charts which John discovered were in Glenn's handwriting.

By 1974, he had moved on to Long Beach State University where he met Dan Barrett, who, as Dan has done in so many instances for countless individuals, recommended John to the booking folks at Disneyland.

For the next five years, John was a member of the Banjo Kings. "As a 20-year-old novice, the best advice I got at Disney was to show up and shut up," he recalled. "I learned over 100 tunes from Sonny Helmer and acquired a show business attitude." He later took lessons from George Smith, whose claim to fame was that he had subbed for the great Eddie Lang.

The early '80s found John playing with the Rhythm Boys at the Bonaventure Hotel in Los Angeles where one night the daughter of Harry Barris (one of Paul Whiteman's original Rhythm Boys) came in to hear the trio. 1984 was the start of a highly-successful, 10-year run with the Palm Springs Yacht Club whose members included Lee "Westy" Westenhofer, Bob Reitmeier and Matt Johnson. The quartet played clubs, festivals and private parties and frequently opened for headliners like Julie Andrews, Rich Little, Andy Williams and the Smothers Brothers. Combining the right mix of humor and music, John and "Westy" had a routine where they did a duet of *Edelweiss* (from *Sound of Music)* in which their only instruments were their hands.

John worked for six years as an animation designer and kept his hand in music free-lancing with such bands as Janet Klein & Her Parlor Boys and a vintage dance orchestra led by Johnny Crawford, who co-starred with Chuck Connors in "The Rifleman". In 2011, John was back at Disneyland with the Rhythm Rascals.

John plays a beautiful silver National steel guitar (also known as a resonator guitar) that is a replica of a 1926 model. The National String Instrument Corporation of Los Angeles (1926-32) manufactured the first resonating guitar, described as having a tone like a banjo and guitar and similar in concept to the dobro used by some country-western musicians. Although the two instruments are played differently, they are now made by the same company.

John, who sings, whistles and occasionally plays the kazoo, is an admirer of Jim Kweskin, founder of the Jim Kweskin Jug Band that successfully modernized the sound of pre-World War II rural music. He is partial to old clothing and loves to create the image of a Dapper Dan from the Jazz Age.

The Ellis Island Boys at Disneyland
Bryan Shaw, Ralph Reynolds, Katie Cavera and John Reynolds

The Rascals have gone through a series of name changes and are now the Ellis Island Boys. As for how the latest moniker evolved, Ralf explains, "At Disney, there is a story behind everything. The Paradise Garden Bandstand where we play is considered an 'international bandstand' where several bands play different styles of music from

136

around the world. So we were supposed to have met at Ellis Island, the New York gateway for millions of immigrants to the United States. Because we all loved American music, we formed a band and moved to California to perform this music that we so love."

All members of the band, which includes Nate Ketner on alto sax and Katie Cavera on string bass, wear ZaSu hats, which are akin to newsboy or Gatsby caps. Ralf has been designing and producing this style of headwear for 35 years. It takes him two and a half hours to make one, and through the ZaSu Company, he has been selling 450-500 a year through eBay at $70 per hat. He admits he once had a garage full of sewing machines, but the number has greatly reduced as he and his wife Gladys have made trips to her native Honduras to teach those in need of clothing how to sew. Ralf once had a collection of 80 military motorcycles, but now has only two, the license plate on one of which reads ZASU.

But like their grandmother, the Reynolds brothers get their greatest enjoyment from entertaining and making people smile. "We strive to have a good time and want the audience to have a good time, which makes it all worthwhile. Smiling is contagious. We put a lot of energy into our shows, but we never use a predetermined set of tunes. We'll be playing a number, and one of the band members thinks of a song, we'll just pick it up from there. It's very spontaneous."

SCOTT ROBINSON
Futuristic Jazzman

Published April 2016

A highly-respected performer in all areas of jazz from traditional to avant-garde, **Scott Robinson** has established his own unique musical voice, which was described in a Northsea Jazz Festival program as "combining solid foundations with great daring." The headline in a *Wall Street Journal* article by Will Friedwald tabbed him "Jazz Futurist, Mad Scientist."

"What planet did this guy come from?" is how Benny Goodman reacted when he heard legendary cornetist Bix Beiderbecke for the first time. Trumpeter Randy Sandke has been known to use that same line to introduce Scott. As Will Friedwald pointed out in his WSJ article, "There's no one else doing anything close to what Mr. Robinson is doing: playing every style that exists in the jazz world, on almost every horn known to man, and even some rhythm instruments."

Primarily a tenor saxophonist (he ranked second after Sonny Rollins in a *Downbeat* poll), Scott is considered one of today's most wide-ranging instrumentalists. He has been heard on tenor sax with Buck Clayton's band and Jon-Erik Kellso's EarRegulars, on trumpet with Lionel Hampton's quintet, on alto clarinet with Paquito D'Rivera's clarinet quintet, on baritone sax with Maria Schneider or the New York City Opera Orchestra, and in an outer-space jam session with musicians from the Sun Ra Arkestra where he'll bring out some of his really far-out horns from his collection of unusual and obscure instruments. For example, he owns and records with a vintage contrabass saxophone, so rare that fewer than 20 are known to exist in playable condition.

A busy traveler, Scott has performed in more than 40 countries, once touring five continents in a three-month period. He has played for the King of Thailand and at U.S. presidential inaugurals, and in such diverse and prestigious venues as Carnegie Hall, the Village Vanguard, Library of Congress and the Vienna Opera House. His band, the Doctette, an outfit inspired by the 1930s and '40s pulp-fiction character Doc Savage, has played at the Newport Jazz Festival.

His many works as a composer cover a wide range, from solo performance pieces, jazz tunes, chamber works on up to large-scale compositions for wind bands and symphony orchestras. He has been recorded on more than 200 LP and CD releases, including over a dozen on which he was the leader, and two of which won GRAMMY Awards. He has received four fellowships from the National Endowment for the Arts.

The son of a piano teacher and a writer for *National Geographic Books*, Scott grew up in an 18th Century farmhouse in Virginia. When he was quite young, he and his brother David organized a small-folks Tijuana Brass band. While in high school, he received the Louis Armstrong Award along with the Best Soloist Award from the

National Association of Jazz Educators. He graduated from Berklee College of Music in 1981, and the next year, became the College's youngest faculty member up to that time.

In 2000, the U.S. State Department named Robinson "Jazz Ambassador" and funded a 2001 tour of West Africa that covered 11 countries where he played the early works of Louis Armstrong. Arbors Records subsequently released an album from these appearances.

At his New Jersey residence, Scott has constructed a studio/laboratory (The Temple of Sound) for sonic research and creating recordings for the "World of Tomorrow through Sound." ScienSonic Laboratories, which is reported guarded by Scott's pet rabbit, has been recognized by the Space Foundation for its Certified Space Imagination Products. His albums carry a sticker proclaiming "WARNING: This Music takes place in another world. Conditions may be hazardous."

Again quoting Will Friedwald, "Mr. Robinson's 'laboratory' is a converted garage behind his Teaneck home where he stores his working instruments. Thousands of additional parts and incomplete horns are stashed in his basement."

"Lanky, bearded and bespectacled, Mr. Robinson plays up the idea of looking and acting like a Mad Scientist of Jazz. He has a custom lab coat that he wears to his own gigs and hands out specially-made test tubes as souvenirs. Although comfortable in the jazz past, his ScienSonic projects are distinctly futuristic and avant-garde, starting with the album covers which feature paintings from 1950s science-fiction paperbacks by the late Richard Powers.

Scott acknowledges that "the music we do for ScienSonic is unabashedly, unapologetically forward-thinking. It's not for everyone – but it's for any one. I try to keep a balance in my life. I still love to play beautiful melodies, old tunes, ballads. I never want to so far out that I can't play *Stardust.*"

Scott's older brother David perhaps says it best: "He's a genius. He plays the entire spectrum of jazz from trad to free-form with equal mastery, and he plays all the reeds and all the brass superbly, not to mention theremin and other non-wind instruments. He's an adventurous soul who invests all of himself in every musical situation. He's also quite an intellectual, yet he's never outgrown his childhood sense of wonder and humor. He has created an astonishing body of original compositions from jazz tunes to symphonic works. I love him dearly, and I can't believe he's my brother."

*(The **theremin** is an electronic musical instrument controlled without physical contact by the thereminist (performer). It is named after its inventor, Leon Theremin, who patented the device in 1928.)*

THE FAMILY CIRCUS.   **By Bil Keane**

"Just what I wanted — a faxophone!"

RANDY SANDKE
A Multifaceted Talent

Published September 2017

Versatility and innovation are two terms that most appropriately can be applied to trumpeter **Randy Sandke**, although he considers himself more of a survivor who has been able to make a living playing music since he had to turn down an offer to play in Janis Joplin's band because he had developed a hernia of the throat which made it uncomfortable for him to play the trumpet.

Growing up in Chicago where his father was a college professor and his mother an amateur pianist. Randy and his older brother Jordan discovered some 78rpm records his parents had and were soon immersed in listening to Armstrong, Beiderbecke and Miles Davis. While Randy says, "These jazz legends had a lasting effect on us both, and while traditional jazz was my first love, it wasn't long before I was listening to the likes of Clifford Brown and Dizzy Gillespie."

The Sandke brothers took a shot at playing the drums, but when Jordan brought home a trumpet, Randy knew he has found his instrument. It was while playing for dances and private parties in his early teens that Randy realized his father's life as a professor was rather confining, and "the idea of traveling around and playing music seemed like the most thrilling lifestyle I could imagine."

While attending the University of Chicago Laboratory School, he won a stage band competition that entitled him to attend a two-week summer school course on arranging taught by Oliver Nelson at Indiana University. That fall, he enrolled at IU as a composition major. In 1967 and 1968, he attracted national attention at the Notre Dame Collegiate Jazz Festival, where Dan Morgenstern, the iconic *Downbeat* editor, had high praise for "the most original, creative and stimulating combo jazz heard at the Festival" and identified the leader of the septet as "a trumpeter with great promise, combining a fine, bright tone and flawless execution with real musical intelligence."

During his time at Indiana, Randy played in a variety of groups, the most popular of which was Mrs. Seaman's Sound Band. The Mrs. Seaman in question was in charge of one of the student dining facilities on campus. "Her passion was throwing people out of the dining hall who weren't properly attired. We were always at each other's throats, so we named the band after her."

Randy was playing his horn at a high level, especially when competing with the amplified rock sounds commonly heard around campus, which exacerbated some flaws in his technique and almost cost him his career. As he explains, "I had teachers when I was young, but I was bullheaded and thought I could teach myself to play since most of my heroes were self-taught musicians. But the trumpet is very unforgiving, and if you don't do it right, it becomes your worst enemy."

Attempting to play became more difficult, and it was determined he had a hernia in his throat. He was in Chicago consulting a doctor about an operation when he received the call from Janis Joplin. He said he would love to join her band, but he had this throat problem, to which her response was, "What are you, some kind of hypochondriac?"

Sandke had the operation, but was unsure of the cause of his problem, so at the age of 19, he put away his horn and did not pick it up again for the next 10 years. During this interim, he spent three years as piano accompanist for the dance department at a women's college in Vermont, moved to New York City to work for ASCAP, did some teaching, and played guitar in funk bands and for singers on the cabaret circuit. However, he didn't feel fulfilled and contemplated giving up music as a career.

Then along came a trumpet-playing friend from Indiana who moved into his apartment and convinced Randy, with his help and lessons from Vincent Penzerella (NY Philharmonic, Met Opera, Broadway shows, Lester Lanin), that he could and would play the trumpet again at a high level of competency.

Randy virtually had to relearn his instrument, but within six months, the work and study paid off, and he began getting gigs. "There were times I know I sounded pretty terrible, but New York is the fastest place to learn because you're working with good players. My endurance and range improved to the point I felt I was playing better than I ever had before the operation."

His first job was subbing for his brother in Vince Giordano's Nighthawks, an association that lasted for five years. Then Billy Butterfield got sick, and he subbed for him on a tour. He worked at Eddie Condon's Jazz Club, played with Bob Wilber on the *Cotton Club* film soundtrack and in Wilber's Bechet Legacy band, and in the mid-1980s was in bands headed by two of the giants of Swing: Benny Goodman and Buck Clayton.

Over the years he has played and recorded with the best in the business, toured the world, and been a soloist at Carnegie Hall over a dozen times. As a composer, he has had his compositions performed by the likes of the Bulgarian National Orchestra and the Carnegie Hall Jazz Band. He has written arrangements for Sting, Elton John and the King of Thailand and done transcriptions for Wynton Marsalis and the Lincoln Center Jazz Orchestra.

One of the books he has written, *Harmony for a New Millennium*, details a method for exploring non-tonal harmony in the context of both composition and improvisation. "There's a wealth of harmonic combinations that haven't yet made their way into the jazz vocabulary. Metatonal harmony bridges the gap between the language of contemporary classical music and jazz."

Randy has long resisted being typecast musically, saying, "If you grow up playing nothing but modern jazz and shift to a more traditional style, you have to dispense with a lot of your favorite harmonic and rhythmic tricks. Instead, the interest has to come from somewhere else – from melody, phrasing, the sheer sound of your instrument. But I believe those are virtues that can be applied to any style – traditional or modern – and when you do it, you end up with better music."

His other book, *Where the Dark and the Light Folks Meet: Race and the Mythology, Politics and Business of Jazz,* tackled a controversial topic that hit a nerve in the opinion of some people regarding racial integration and socialization of musicians in jazz. The focus of the book discusses how blacks and whites have interacted throughout jazz history, and how the music and society in general has benefited from this interracial contact. He quotes Milt Hinton, an African-

145

American bass player, who says, "Jazz players were integrating way before society decided to do that."

"You have to walk a fine line when discussing racial matters, and as I point out in the book, almost anything you say is likely to offend someone," according to Randy. "To me, these difficulties underscore the timeliness and necessity for frankly discussing these issues. I don't deny that jazz originally came from a black environment, and the majority of its greatest exponents have been African-American. For me and most white jazz musicians, we grew up idolizing so many great African-American musicians. They were our heroes and mentors. But I don't like to see their memory and artistic legacy manipulated to promote a separatist agenda. I don't think that's what they stood for, or what jazz should stand for either."

Considered one of the most eclectic figures in the jazz scene over the past 40 years, Randy Sandke is comfortable in any jazz idiom and acknowledges he feels fortunate to have been able to play with so many great musicians. He is steeped in early jazz and is a true scholar of the work of Louis Armstrong and Bix Beiderbecke. By the same token, he is equally committed to creating his own challenging music, both as an instrumentalist and composer, and he always swings. As a researcher and writer, he is unafraid to explore controversial topics and to promote views that may not always be popular and universally accepted.

CYNTHIA SAYER
Doing What She Loves

Published October 2017

It's your turn in a tense game of Trivial Pursuit, and the question is: *Who was the official banjoist for the New York Yankees?*

Or you might be asked: *What member of the National 4-String Banjo Hall of Fame was the piano player in Woody Allen's New Orleans Jazz Band?*

The questions get tougher: *Who is the only banjoist to have graced the stage of the Metropolitan Opera concert hall and to have performed with the New York Philharmonic Orchestra?*

And finally: *Who published a play-along book with CD downloads for people seeking to learn and practice traditional hot jazz and swing?*

The answer to all of the above: **Cynthia Sayer.**

Cynthia Sayer has made a career out of doing something she loves. She originally wanted to play the drums, but when she was 13, her parents bribed her with a banjo and lessons as a more peaceful pursuit. This happenstance put her on a career path that has led to work in films, stints with symphony orchestras, performances at the White House and Carnegie Hall, teaching, and extensive international touring.

As a magna cum laude graduate from Ithaca College with a bachelor's degree in English, she thought about going to law school to become a lawyer, but decided to give music a shot for a year or two. She kept extending that "year or two," and it wasn't long before she concluded there's nothing wrong with earning your living at something you love doing.

She was soon playing with such legendary artists as Bucky Pizzarelli, Dick Hyman, Les Paul, Marvin Hamlisch, Wynton Marsalis and Wycliffe Gordon. Her extensive career includes performing for two U.S. Presidents (once at the White House), playing banjo, ukulele and

147

piano on feature film and TV soundtracks including several Woody Allen films, and doing TV commercials and radio jingles.

She tours with her bands: Cynthia Sayer & Joyride, Cynthia Sayer & Sparks Fly, and Cynthia Sayer's Women of the World Jazz Band (WOW). Her albums included *Attractions* with Bucky Pizzarelli and *Joyride* with Charlie Giordana, a member of Bruce Springsteen's E Street Band. In 2006, she was inducted into the National Four-String Banjo Hall of Fame, which is part of the American Banjo Museum in Oklahoma City.

She was featured on the PBS television documentary *Give Me the Banjo* that brought together contemporary players with folklorists, historians, instrument makers and passionate amateurs to tell the story of America's instrument in all its richness and diversity.

She was a founding member of Woody Allen's New Orleans Jazz Band and was its pianist for over 10 years. "When I was first approached, I wondered why they would ask me when there are a ton of great piano players in New York City. I'm better on banjo. However,, I realized that Woody was partial to the clarinet style of George Lewis, and the band was like a George Lewis-Bunk Johnson New Orleans-style band, which has a very particular kind of sound. I loved the band and did play banjo on occasion when Eddy Davis, the regular banjo player, couldn't make it."

"I didn't know about the Trivial Pursuit question until a friend told me about it. What happened was that I was in the "A Band" that played for certain home games at Yankee Stadium as well as for some Yankee special events. I'm not a big sports fan, but got to meet a few players. It was cool."

Cynthia has also been active as an educator, performing programs about early jazz and the 4-string banjo at colleges, giving lectures/demonstrations for various organizations, teaching workshops while on tour worldwide, giving private lessons, hosting jam sessions, and writing feature articles for several American and British trade publications.

Dispelling all the bad jokes about banjos and people who play the instrument, Cynthia gave a lecture at the Lincoln Center Jazz Academy entitled THE VENERABLE JAZZ BANJO: Stars & Music from Speakeasies, Vaudeville, Concert Halls and More. While people normally associate the banjo with bluegrass, folk and country music, Cynthia pointed out that it was the 4-string jazz banjo that defined the hot rhythm section sound of American pop music of the Roaring '20s and early '30s

As for the play-along book, which is titled You're in The Band, she said, "My students had expressed a good deal of frustration over the years in trying to find the right kind of play-along materials. They asked me to put something together, but I was always too busy with gigs and other work. Finally the time was right."

"Once I conceived the project, it grew organically to be more involved than I thought it would be. It's designed to give a genuine experience of what it's like to play in a hot jazz, trad-style group and is for all jazz instruments, not just the banjo. Bria Skonberg (trumpet), Mike Weatherly (string bass) and Kevin Dorn (drums) recorded 13 familiar tunes with me."

"Each tune is performed at two different speeds: practice or gig tempo, and we leave space for the musician to play along. The book gives lots of helpful information and tips. The *You're in the Band* package will help players learn real traditional jazz by utilizing accurate music, playing styles and tempos as are played on quality professional gigs today – and to have fun in the process!"

There's no question in Cynthia Sayer's mind that she made the right decision to become a musician instead of a barrister, and that she picked the right instrument on which to build her career. "The banjo is in the midst of an enormous renaissance, and there is some great talent out there. It is seriously cool to be a banjo player right now. Needless to say, I'm happy about that."

"I remember when I was in my 20s, and I would go to parties, and people would say to me, 'Oh, what do you do,' and I would say, 'I play the banjo,' and they would look at me and literally not know how to respond. It was just not part of the consciousness of my generation. Now if I say I play the banjo, everyone is like, 'Wow, that's so cool!'"

Mark Twain had that figured out 150 years ago when he wrote in volume 2 of his "Early Tales and Sketches," *"The piano may do for lovesick girls who lace themselves to skeletons, and lunch on chalk, pickles, and slate pencils. But give me the banjo... When you want genuine music— music that will come right home to you like a bad quarter, suffuse your system like strychnine whiskey…ramify your whole constitution like the measles, and break out on your hide like the pin-feather pimples on a picked goose—when you want all this, just smash your piano, and invoke the glory-beaming banjo!"*

BOB SCHULZ
From Teaching to Carnegie Hall

Published August 2014

Bob Schulz is one of the more popular musicians on the jazz festival/jazz party circuit. He plays a great horn in the style of Bob Scobey. He has a more than pleasant singing voice in the tradition of Clancy Hayes, Scobey's banjoist. His ever-ready smile and congenial personality make him a big fan favorite whenever and wherever he appears. During the decade of the 1990s, he was consistently voted the #1 cornetist and ranked third on the list of vocalists by traditional jazz fans in an annual poll.

A native of Wonewoc, Wisconsin (58 miles north of Madison near the Wisconsin Dells), he spent 17 years as a teacher and band director before joining the legendary Turk Murphy Jazz Band in San Francisco in 1979. He was with Murphy for eight years during which time he participated in 300 taped radio shows, recorded many LPs, and toured the United States and Europe. A highlight was the sold-out Carnegie Hall tribute to Turk where at one time there were as many as 200 musicians and fans on stage honoring the terminally-ill leader. Following Murphy's passing in 1987, Bob free-lanced in San Francisco before forming his Frisco Jazz Band in 1990.

Growing up, Bob would hear his mother sing during family gatherings, and his brother and two sisters all played the piano and their father's cornet. Bob was the one who eventually inherited the cornet that had been passed down in the family. He was a four-sport athlete in high school as well as playing in the band and singing in the chorus, "The band director gave lessons to all the kids in the music program," Bob recalled, "I never had private lessons beyond that. During the summers, we had Saturday night band concerts, and I along with my brother and a friend (who later was in Horace Heidt's original band) would play triple-tonguing trumpet trios. It was a great experience."

Bob Schulz at the Bunny Berigan Jazz Jubilee in Wisconsin

Bob attended the University of Wisconsin-LaCrosse, intending to be an athletic coach, but after the first semester, decided that music and working with young people was to be his future career. The college did not have a music major, so his concentration was in social studies, with music and biology minors. He later attended UW-Madison summers to receive his master's in music.

His first job in 1961 was teaching general music and world history for grades 1-8, plus band and chorus, for an annual salary of $4,200. After seven years, he moved to another community where for the next decade he worked with the school bands (including the marching band), gave lessons and started a jazz ensemble. His bands consistently took top honors in concert band competitions and in 1975, represented the State of Wisconsin at Disney World during the country's Bicentennial celebration.

"Some people say teaching is boring," he said. "No way, because it's always different. You're dealing with different kids and different assignments all the time. When I taught general music classes, I had to sing all the time because I couldn't play the piano. If you found a way to motivate kids, you've got them hooked. Those 17 years were one of the true high points of my life."

One former student, who later went on the road with Clyde McCoy, remembered Bob as an excellent teacher, saying "Some instructors were very good on one instrument, but weak on others. Bob had a good grasp of all the instruments, plus that rare charisma along with a handsome boyish look and fine stage presence. He always led by example and really cared about each and every student. I didn't fully appreciate then how great he was and what a good basic musical education he gave us."

In the summer of 1962, Bob was assigned to Fort Lewis, Washington with the Army National Guard 32nd Division band. "We pretty much just played concerts, including a reception for astronaut John Glenn. All the guys in the band were pros, so working with them was a real pleasure. During this summer, we formed the Riverboat Ramblers, which was my introduction to Dixieland. When we got back to Wisconsin, we kept the Ramblers going."

In 1979, the Ramblers were playing at the St. Louis Ragtime Festival on the Goldenrod Showboat along with Turk's band, the Salty Dogs, Jim Cullum's Happy Jazz Band, Ernie Carson's Castle JB and a few others. In telling 'the rest of the story' of how he joined Murphy, Bob recounts that after a few gin and tonics, Ernie Carson talked him into sitting in with the Salty Dogs on the River Barge. "We both put paper bags over our heads and played a tune or two with the Dogs. I don't know where Turk's vantage point was during all of this, but since he needed a horn player, and on John Gill's recommendation, he apparently was sufficiently impressed that he decided to give me a try."

"I got a letter a week later offering me a job with his band at Earthquake McGoon's in San Francisco – 50 bucks a night, $250 a week. I had just gone through a divorce and was still teaching. I asked for a leave of absence, but was turned down. But I didn't want to pass up the opportunity, so I resigned my teaching position and moved to California. My eight years with Turk were great. I learned a lot about being a leader as well as a sideman. He was a tough nut, but you always knew where you stood with him. McGoon's is where I met my current wife, Linda, who was a waitress here."

Turk Murphy was best man at Linda and Bob's wedding 33 years ago, which produces another 'rest of the story' episode. It was a late summer day in 1981. The ceremony was to take place in the yard of her parents' home under a stately oak tree. As the ceremony proceeded, the minister intoned, "If anyone here objects to this union, speak now or forever hold your peace." Bob realized something was up because that phrase wasn't usually included in most wedding ceremonies.

Suddenly, over the hill and down the driveway roars a 1920s convertible roadster loaded with some McGoon patrons known as the Lato Mob, dressed in 20s attire and firing toy machine guns. They jump out of the car shouting, "Stop the wedding. Dutch Schulz is wanted by the authorities in Chicago." They produce an actual photo of Schultz the gangster, which fortunately bore little resemblance to Schulz the bridegroom. This performance was obviously setup by Turk, a known prankster, and instantly changed the seriousness of the occasion.

With the demise of the Murphy band, Bob teamed up with Jim Maihack as a nine-month replacement for the Don Neely Quintet at the San Francisco Fairmont Hotel and then signed on with Neely for the next three years. In 1990, he recruited Bill Napier, Bob Mielke, Ray Skjelbred, Bill Carroll, John Gill and Wayne Jones to form the Frisco Jazz Band. In 1988, he began a long association with Scott Anthony and his Golden Gate Rhythm Machine.

Bob occasionally leads the Turk Murphy Alumni Band for special engagements and is also a member of the Lost Weekend Western swing band. During a recording session with the San Francisco Starlight Orchestra in the early 1990s, Bob had the opportunity to play a cornet once owned by Bix Beiderbecke – the one owned by Robert Christiansen. "It was neat to be able to play it," he explained. "It was very free-blowing and open, but to me, it was a little stiff. I couldn't play it for an extended period."

When not on the bandstand, Bob at age 76 enjoys gardening, biking and refinishing furniture. Since 1975, he has collected Lionel trains, and his collection now numbers in the hundreds. He even has a water tower and a 17-foot signal tower in his backyard.

Summing up his long career, he concluded, "As a cornetist, I always try to play a pleasing tone and to keep it simple. I've been fortunate to use my God-given talent and to play without a lot of effort, because I don't practice very much. I've been over some bumpy roads – as I'm sure we all have, but overall, I have to say I've been lucky in life, which shows somebody up there must like me."

JOHN SHERIDAN
A Musician of Impeccable Taste

Published February 2014

It could arguably be said that **John Sheridan** has spent more time in his 40-year professional career backing up and arranging for jazz cornetists than any pianist in recent memory. He is best known for his 26-year association with the Jim Cullum band, for whom he has contributed more than 800 charts as an arranger. Writing about Sheridan in 2002, the late Cam Miller referred to the classically-trained pianist as "the straw that stirs the drink" for the popular San Antonio band.

John's musical odyssey stared typically with piano lessons at the age of 8 in his home town of Columbus, Ohio. When his father brought home a recording of the famous Benny Goodman 1938 Carnegie Hall concert, his interest temporary switched to the clarinet. At the age of 10, he found himself debating whether he should sound like BG or Artie Shaw.

"While Benny was my first inspiration, I became equally enthralled with Artie Shaw," John recalled. "They both were extremely talented and difficult personalities. Artie had more facets to his talent. He wrote great arrangements, which Benny didn't. Artie's band reflected his musical ideas more than Benny's band did."

"Benny, on the other hand, was a catalyst who brought together many individual talents and propelled them to great careers. Artie couldn't do that because he was always getting disillusioned and running off to Mexico. In the end, they were both fascinating people who created tons of great music and inspired me at a time when I was young and impressionable and needed direction."

John played clarinet in junior and senior high school, but said, "It became apparent that my skills were more suited for the piano, and I realized that I was never going to be able to play like Benny Goodman or Artie Shaw."

With Teddy Wilson and Jess Stacy as his models, he began his performing career at the age of 13 when he joined five classmates to form The Novelaires, a group that for the next five years, played for dances, conventions, country fairs, even on a Cincinnati television show. "Our first job paid five dollars, and I made $1.25," John chuckled. On one occasion, they shared billing with cornetist Bobby Hackett, which was a big thrill for the young boys. Just as they were about to start their second set, they were hustled off the stage by a nervous parent to be confronted by the vice squad and charged with being underage at an establishment that served liquor.

Following graduation from high school, he enrolled at Capital University in Columbus as a music major and gained further experience as accompanist for the college glee club and rehearsal pianist for the Kenly Players. With his degree in hand and the Vietnam Conflict still raging in 1968, he signed on with the U.S. Navy

School of Music and was assigned to be the combo pianist for the Navy Band in Washington, D.C.

"I did my first serious arranging at that time," Sheridan said. I subbed quite a bit for The Commodores and did some gigs on the Presidential yacht, the Sequoia. It was during President Nixon's first administration. He only used the yacht as a getaway when he needed to prepare for an important speech or summit meeting. But he did let his favorite congressmen and Cabinet members use it for entertaining. I was like a fly on the wall watching a slice of history, and everyone was super nice."

John had a career decision to make when he was discharged from the Navy in 1972. A Navy friend suggested he join him in Dallas where John was able to work on his Master's degree at North Texas State (now the University of North Texas). He soon had a busy musician-student schedule that included work with Tommy Loy's Upper Dallas Jazz Band.

He completed his Master of Music degree in 1977, with emphasis on music theory. "Even though I had done arranging while in the Navy," he explained, "I became much more proficient while at North Texas. What was most important was learning how to arrange and orchestrate when not sitting at the piano. It's fascinating moving little black dots around on a piece of paper and knowing that they correspond to certain sounds."

The Tommy Loy band played at a place called The Railhead. In 1976, the Cullum band stopped in after playing a gig at a local country club. "They listened to us and then played, and we had a regular battle-of-the-bands. Later in the evening, Jim got me off in a corner and said his pianist was getting along in years and probably would retire in the foreseeable future. He asked if I would be interested when that happened."

That call came in late 1978, and John joined the Cullum band in San Antonio in April of 1979, which he describes as "the best thing that ever happened to me." His predecessor had done all of the band's arrangements, so John easily stepped into that role. It was a demanding schedule with the band playing six nights a week, recording, traveling, and doing the weekly *Riverwalk Live on the Landing* syndicated programs that were heard on 200 Public Radio International affiliates.

At the end of 2002, he decided to take a break "to do something different," which included extensive recordings of his own "Dream Band" with vocalist Rebecca Kilgore. He returned to the Cullum band on a full-time basis in 2011.

Sheridan's interest in arranging stemmed from hearing Fletcher Henderson's arrangements for the Goodman band. "You most closely identify with the artists you hear first, which is why Fletcher, Teddy and Jess still influence my arranging and playing. Bob Haggart was also a wonderful teacher," he stated. John arranged the Cullum band's critically-acclaimed CBS Masterworks release of *Porgy and Bess* as well as for the CDs in the Riverwalk Vintage Jazz Collection. His two-piano duets with Dick Hyman are among his favorites.

John Sheridan has been referred to as "a musician of impeccable taste." While he has been influenced by many of the legendary jazz piano players from years past, he says, "I don't try to sound like anyone else. Each of us is making a statement within a particular style from different periods. It's all jazz!" He is a great dog lover and an inveterate fan of Ohio State football, even to the point of having a Buckeye Shrine in his home. He concluded our conversation, saying, "I love what I'm doing and don't plan to retire any time soon."

SIDE STREET STRUTTERS
"Proud of What We Do"

Vince and Rob Verdi's father was a schoolteacher in Ossining, NY and a self-taught drummer. Each summer he would take a sabbatical and enroll in courses related to vocational education and industrial arts. He would usually bring the family along, and one summer they made the cross-country trek to Arizona. When it came time to attend college, both boys opted for Arizona State University. Vince graduated in 1980 with an undergraduate degree in Education and later earned a Master's degree in Business Management. Rob came along four years later to major in Music Education.

It was in 1983 while in college that the boys formed the Side Street Stutters as a way to pick up a little beer-and-pizza money. The band name came from observing the many side streets in Old Town Scottsdale as they would drive north on Scottsdale Road from the University in Tempe. A year later, the Strutters won the Southern Comfort competition (at which Clark Terry and Tommy Newsome were two of the judges) as the nation's top collegiate Dixieland band.

This resulted in a three-week national tour and appearances on the Merv Griffin Show, Jerry Lewis Telethon and the Today Show, all of which brought them to the attention of the folks who book talent at Disneyland in California. An offer to perform weekends was forthcoming, but the problem was that a couple of the musicians were still in college, and two others had taken teaching jobs.

The Verdis recalled, "We were all young and single, and the Disneyland offer looked pretty good. So until the other guys graduated, we would take the red-eye and commute every weekend from Phoenix to Orange County – at our own expense. That summer it became a full-time job, and we all moved to California. We replaced the Jazz Minors who had played there for the previous four years."

For the next 22 years (1985-2006), they played at Disneyland year-round with intermittent breaks to tour. "We did strolling performances, popping in and out of shops or going into restaurants as well as doing stage shows at New Orleans Square. It got a bit boring at times when it seemed that every fifth request was for *It's a Small World After All*. But no matter how many times we played a tune, we always made sure that the audience was having a great experience. It didn't take us long to realize that Disneyland was a whole lot better than working in a smoky club, and we knew we always had a guaranteed audience."

In those early years, the band represented the United States at the Cervantino International Music & Arts Festival in Mexico; won first place in an International Association of Jazz Educators-sponsored competition; and took top honors at the prestigious Breda International Jazz Festival in Holland, the first American band to do so in the Festival's history up to that time. Their artistic accomplishments were recognized by the National Endowment for the Arts and the United States Information Agency, and they performed at the White House for President and Mrs. Reagan.

Over the years, the Strutters have presented hundreds of concerts and school outreach programs in 49 states and nine foreign countries. Along with their standard repertoire, they can present theme shows that include *Back to Bourbon Street, Jumping into Swing, Shiny Stockings* which features vocalist Meloney Collins; and *Winter Wonderland* for the holiday season.

With their three decades of performing and teaching experience, the Strutters have developed comprehensive jazz outreach programs customized for each academic and age level. The band will demonstrate various instruments and jazz styles, introduce the students to simple melodic, harmonic and rhythmic concepts in a light-hearted way, include a bit of jazz history and vintage video, and always encourage audience participation.

Co-leader Rob Verde shows off this six-foot contrabass saxophone. Also pictured are band members Curtis Brengle, Bruce Lett and Paul Johnson. Missing are co-leader Vince Verde, Greg Varlotta, Roger Bissell and vocalist Meloney Collins.

Rob, who is the band's artistic director and master of ceremonies, continues to be a regular performer at Disneyland, conducting jazz workshops for the Disney Magic Music Days Guest Talent program, as well as participating in a variety of musical ensembles and projects in the Los Angeles area. His passion for collecting saxophones has resulted in a collection of over 100 saxes along with 150 rare wind, brass, and percussion instruments. In 2008, he was featured playing his 6 ½-foot-tall contrabass sax on the soundtrack of *Horton Hears A Who*.

His *Saxophobia* show offers a unique glimpse at some of the most unusual saxophones ever manufactured and the classic melodies that popularized this warmly embraced and versatile musical instrument. The show explores over a half century of jazz classics and recognizes the musical contributions of such artists as Stan Getz, Sidney Bechet, Charlie Parker, Paul Desmond, Gerry Mulligan, John

162

Coltrane, Frank Trambauer and others. Audiences are introduced to over a dozen variations of Adolphe Sax's 1846 invention, including a curved sopranino, plastic alto, straight tenor, connosax, slide sax, bass and the rare six-foot contrabass sax.

Vince Verdi, whose hobby is cabinetmaking and woodworking, serves as business manager and tour director for the band and deals with the presenters. In 2010, he accepted a position with Live On Stage, an industry leader based in Nashville, Tenn. that presents talent to community concert organizations. He represents the company in a string of East Coast states running from Pennsylvania to Florida and works with three dozen communities that Live On Stage serves in bringing live arts performances into these cities.

The Strutters have recorded a dozen CDs and DVDs, and their versatile repertoire spans musical decades from early New Orleans Dixieland and blues to the Big Band sounds of Ellington and Goodman to the classic Great American Songbook of Berlin and Gershwin to current pop tunes. As the band has matured and became much more businesslike and professional, the Verdi brothers acknowledge that they have been fortunate in having had fairly stable personnel over the years. Greg Varlotta, the tap-dancing trumpeter from Lockport, Illinois, was one of the original members and is still with the band as well as drummer Paul Johnson who has been playing with the boys since 1985. Although original trombonist Joey Sellers (currently Director of Jazz Studies at Saddleback College) no longer tours with the band, he continues to do arrangements for the Strutters.

The co-leaders concluded, "We've come a long ways since we won the Southern Comfort competition and being a show band with the striped shirts, straw hats and corny jokes. We respect each other and have had very few personality conflicts. We're proud of what we do."

DAVE TATROW
Dual Career Success

Published August 2015

While the great majority of individuals interviewed for this series of musician profiles depend on their jobs as music makers as their main livelihood, **Dave Tatrow** has had two successful careers: one as a town administrator in small Michigan communities for 43 years, and the other for which he is best known to jazz fans across the country as a hard-blowing trumpeter, bandleader and traditional jazz advocate.

But the music came first. Dave was exposed to a lot of old-time music growing up in the Flint area where his grandfather, father and two uncles were self-taught banjo players in local dance bands. So it was natural that he should follow suit, but it took an accident to make it happen. At the age of six on one of his more adventurous days, he fell off a windmill and broke his arm. While recuperating, he decided to take up the banjo and proceeded to learn a few chords. At age 11, he switched to trumpet when he joined the school band.

He had his first paying job on New Year's Eve 1965 at age 15 with his uncle Marston Tatrow and a year later became part of a teen-age dance band that played for weddings and parties. He attended Mott Community College where he studied Public Administration. He worked a couple summers at Dupont Manufacturing where he played in a dance band called the Shades of Blue with his co-workers.

In 1971, he did an apprenticeship in heating and plumbing for a year and then was hired as assistant superintendent of public works for the Village of Otisville, Michigan –population 884. A year later, he became superintendent, and his duties expanded to include administration and budgeting. As he took on more responsibilities, he became the Village's first Village Manager in 1991. During his tenure he created a Downtown Development Authority and was its director/secretary. He also served as zoning administrator and code enforcement officer for the Village.

While maintaining a busy schedule as a village official, music was still an important part of his life. In 1970, he started working in lounges around the Flint/Saginaw area with many established musicians. During that time, he was in an organ trio that played at Bintz's Apple Mountain Ski Lodge in Freeland for five years where he started doing vocals and learned to play the vibraphone. He continued to play lounges until 1979, when he joined the Oppermann brothers and the New Reformation Jazz Band, an association that would last for 21 years.

By 2000, Dave, deciding that it was time to slow down and take some time off from the hectic pace, left the New Reformation Band. A short time later, Dave Fanning, the director of the Suncoast Jazz Festival in Clearwater, Florida, called and asked Dave if he would be interested in putting a group together for their festival that fall. Dave agreed and summoned many of his old band mates from the NRJB along with Randy Morris on piano and Bob Draga on clarinet.

As the Festival approached, Dave Fanning needed to know the name of the band. Finally after many weeks of struggling with dozens of names, Dave received a call from Bob Draga and trombonist Keith Dewitt. Draga had played at a club called Woody Reilly's Warehouse in Largo, Florida and suggested the band be called "Wally's Whorehouse Waifs". That idea was quickly nixed, and Dewitt suggested Wally's Warehouse Waifs. Since then, it's been seven or eight festivals a year, plus a cruise. Dave's wife of 29 years, Cathy, serves as band manager.

In mid-2011 after 39 years on the job, Dave retired as Otisville's Village Manager and took advantage of an opportunity to serve as the part-time Village Manager for Reese, Michigan, a town northeast of Saginaw – population 1,415. So he continues to utilize his experience and familiarity with the infrastructure of town governments. It should come as no surprise that his email address is *docjass@ aol.com*.

Wally's Warehouse Waifs has become known for putting on a 45-minute educational program at schools for students ages 5 to 18, usually in conjunction with a festival, although one time they visited 15 schools while on a 500-mile tour. Describing his approach, Dave said, "Having four grandsons, I recognize the students' limited attention span, so it's important to be in control and encourage participation. It's fast-moving, and there's no quiet-time."

He further expounds his philosophy on the band's website under the heading, "Passing It On," where he states: "As musicians, parents and grandparents, the state of today's music greatly concern us! There is no MUSIC in the lives of our children today. Lots of rhythm and percussion; lots of sex, angst and violence. But no MUSIC!"

"We need to change that! Together we can.!"

"Traditional jazz, a true treasure, is America's only original art form.

166

It has endured for over 100 years because it's QUALITY. It's part of our family 'sing-a-longs.' When you think about it, it's very doubtful that future generations will be singing today's Top 40 around the campfire 30 years from now."

"We need to make our loved ones aware of what they are listening to and encourage them to bring the MELODY back and enjoy this finger-snappin', toe-tappin', happy MUSIC. It is our hope that through exposure to real music, future generations will demand more from the entertainment industry."

So this is why Dave Tatrow can take pride in his dual careers as an effective administrator in his community while presenting good music and quality entertainment at virtually every traditional jazz festival in the United States and exposing young people to OKOM in the process.

RAY TEMPLIN
From Shakey's Pizza to Disneyland

Published March 2014

One of the things that interests and intrigues me most as I have interviewed and written about more than 100 musicians in the past decade is identifying the circumstances and situations that led these individuals down the career path they have taken. I found this to be particularly true in the telling of the 71 years of **Ray Templin**'s life story.

At an early age, Ray was intrigued by the music he heard listening to his Father's records and at family sing-alongs, and wondered "how do they do that?" He got his first set of drums at age 5. When his Mother took him for piano lessons, he was asked "to play something." That "something" turned out to be a self-taught version of the *12th Street Rag*, to which the teacher responded, "I can't do anything for the boy!"

From there, Ray progressed through the usual school bands along with gigging around Chicago and "picking up the technical stuff" while attending the University of Illinois. It was while playing at a club near O'Hare Airport that he met his wife, Trish, whose job at the time was selling flight insurance. They have now been married for 51 years.

With the Vietnam War underway, Ray was drafted into the Army and was assigned to a military police unit in Georgia, but it wasn't long before he was transferred to the Special Service Entertainment Division. During his two-year tour of duty, he was able to moonlight at a nearby Shakey's Pizza Parlor, a chain that had been started in Sacramento by Sherwood "Shakey" Johnson, who was known for his great love of Dixieland jazz.

Back in Chicago following discharge, Ray wrote songs and comedy routines for a folk trio that included his wife, a classically-trained singer. While working days for a publishing company, he did jazz brunches with a quintet. In 1975, he signed on with Bob Schulz's Riverboat Ramblers. But the Templins soon began to tire of the weather in the Windy City, and one February day in 1979 while shoveling snow off the roof of his house, Ray made the decision to move to Los Angeles with the prospect of a job at Disney which had come about through an executive contact recommended by a friend.

Ray soon became a favorite at local jazz clubs, playing both piano and drums, and in 1980, he joined Bob Ringwald's Great Pacific Jazz Band which at the time included such top players as Dick Cary, Bob Havens, Zeke Zachery and Don Nelson (Ozzie's brother). Ringwald was also responsible for getting Ray a job playing three nights a week at Shakey's Pizza Parlor in Burbank.

That call from Disney finally came through in 1981 when he was hired to play ragtime piano on Main Street in Disneyland – the start of a 26-year association with the world-famous theme park. He went on to become the bass drummer in the 16-piece marching band and appeared with the park's various show bands, including the Delta Ramblers and the Strawhatters, alternating between piano and drums, plus vocals.

Ray had become a member of the Screen Actors Guild which enabled him to capitalize on his talent for acting and imitating people's voices in the world of television and commercials. At Fantasyland, he was the voice of Stromboli in *Pinocchio"s Daring Journey,* and the German circus ringmaster in *Casey Jr.'s Circus Train.* He even recorded his circus ringmaster role in Spanish, even though he doesn't speak the language by working it out phonetically. He also voiced characters for The Muppets and the sitcom, *Married. . .with Children*

He appeared in 11 episodes of the NBC-TV's *Matlock* series starring Andy Griffith over three seasons. Originally a Southern gospel singer, Griffith liked to integrate music in his films. In the *Andy Griffith Show,* there are many scenes of Andy sitting on the front porch of his home in Mayberry strumming his guitar and singing.

The plot for *Matlock* originally had Andy's lawyer-character appearing either in the courtroom or his office. Griffith wanted another setting, particularly one that featured music. The decision was made to have a nightclub where Andy could occasionally relax or bring clients. The producer rented a nightclub and named it "Ray Templin's Piano Bar." They even built a sign for the front of the building which they used for exterior shots.

Andy would visit Ray's Bar, and there was Ray Templin playing the piano. "Type-casting, indeed!" Ray chuckled. "I never had anything to do with the plot development, but I sure had fun and learned much from that man. Grateful am I." Andy eventually wanted to have the show filmed in North Carolina where he grew up, which brought about the demise of Ray Templin's Piano Bar.

During Ray's years in California he founded or co-founded several bands, including the Palm Springs Yacht Club, Razzmatazz and his Chicagoans, a seven-piece Dixieland group. He has played on over 40 CDs, including one for Yamaha's Artist Series for the Disklavier.

Ray views his years with Disney as "great fun" and recalls that after a day of performing or parading about the park, his face would often be sore from laughing over the crazy antics that happened while entertaining the visitors. As he approached the age of 60, he'd had enough of Los Angeles's traffic-bound commute and decided it was time to retire from the daily hassle. That precipitated a move to Tucson, Arizona with the thought that the warm climate would benefit his wife's rheumatoid arthritis. Now a desert dweller, he continues voice-acting and is the pianist-drummer with one of Arizona's premier classic jazz bands – Wildcat Jazz.

Ray Templin has the relaxed, confident style of an artist who is equally at home before the camera, in the recording studio, and on stage. His versatility, ebullient personality and quick sense of humor has kept him working for nearly 50 years. "My Mother never understood why I wanted to be a professional musician," he said. "Early in my career, she kept asking 'have you had enough?' My answer has always been – and still is - that I've been extremely fortunate to be able to make a living doing what I totally enjoy."

ALLAN VACHE
Hitting the High C's

Published March 2014

VACHE is one of those family names familiar to classic jazz fans where the sons have followed in their father's musical footsteps. Warren Vache Sr. was a bassist, jazz historian, editor and author who was a founder of the New Jersey Jazz Society and the American Federation of Jazz Societies as well as the moving force in establishing the American Jazz Hall of Fame. Sons Warren Jr (cornet and flugelhorn) and Allan (clarinet) rank in the top echelon of today's working musicians.

The elder Vache, whose day job was selling electrical appliances and musical instruments, was an avid record collector, so the boys had an early indoctrination to jazz growing up in Rahway, New Jersey. Both took piano lessons, which Allan calls "a good basis for music." Warren Jr switched to the trumpet in the fourth grade and studied under "Pee Wee" Erwin, who had played in the Benny Goodman and Tommy Dorsey bands and owned a music store in nearby Teaneck.

Allan, who is two years younger than his brother, followed suit when he made the transition to clarinet and later played the baritone saxophone in junior high school. Allan had lessons with the Metropolitan Opera Orchestra's David Dworkin, but his true mentor was the late Kenny Davern. "Kenny was God to me," he said. "He taught me how to play the high notes, and he never stopped being my teacher." Davern was known for his unmatched mastery of the instrument and ability to produce a full-rounded tone in the lower register, combined with highly personal inflections and the ability to hit notes above the conventional range of the clarinet that made his sound immediately recognizable. Even today, Allan uses one of Davern's mouthpieces.

When Allan was in high school, Warren Sr. was playing weekends in Chuck Slate's Traditional Jazz Band, a group that played in the style of the Billy Maxted and Phil Napolian bands. Legends like Bobby Hackett, Gene Krupa, Billy Butterfield or Lou McGarity would sometimes stop by and join in. "I listened to anybody who was good and could really swing," Allan said.

In 1972, he along with trumpeter Randy Reinhart and trombonist Pete Balance (who now plays with the Grove Street Stompers on Monday nights at Arthur's Tavern in Greenwich Village) organized their own band, the Bourbon Street Paraders. The next year, the Vache brothers successfully auditioned for a Broadway musical, *Dr. Jazz*, starring Bobby Van and Lola Falana, with instrumental arrangements written by Dick Hyman and Luther Henderson. After rehearsing for six months, the band, which also included Vince Giordano, John Gill and Sam Pilafian, appeared on stage when the show finally opened. Unfortunately, the production lacked a compelling storyline and closed within a week.

Allan attended Jersey City State College and was performing with the likes of Wild Bill Davison, Max Kaminsky, Clark Terry, Lionel

Hampton, Dick Wellstood and many of the jazz greats of that era. In late 1975 at the age of 21, he was invited to join the Jim Cullum Jazz Band in San Antonio, Texas, the start of a 17-year association. "It was my first time out of the New York metropolitan area and a whole new experience," he recalled. "Jim was always great to me."

In addition to the *Riverwalk, Live from the Landing* shows heard on 200 public radio stations, he traveled extensively with the band throughout North America, Europe and Australia, toured Mexico for the U. S. State Department, and made nine recordings that included the only jazz CD of the entire score of George Gershwin's *Porgy and Bess* folk opera which was released on CBS Masterworks records. Concerts by the Cullum band of *Porgy and Bess* held in such prestigious venues as the Kennedy Center often included the noted bass-baritone William Warfield as narrator. Another highlight was the "Tribute to Turk Murphy" concert at Carnegie Hall in January 1987.

In the summer of 1992, Allan left San Antonio to pursue a free-lance career. He toured England as a soloist, appeared with pop singers Bonnie Rait and Leon Redbone, and can be heard on the soundtrack of the 1998 film, *The Newton Boys*, starring Matthew McConaughey. He moved to Florida in 1993 where for the next eight years, he performed at Walt Disney World, Rosie O'Grady's, Church Street Station and various Orlando attractions.

He was featured in an 18-piece band that toured Brazil as part of a Centennial Tribute to Benny Goodman where he found the classic jazz audiences much younger than in the United States. "It's a matter of exposure," he noted. He is a regular on the jazz party-festival circuit and has recorded extensively on several labels, including 12 CDs for the Nagel-Heyer label based in Hamburg, Germany, six of those as leader.

The smooth sounds Allan Vache produces on his clarinet does indeed invite comparison to a young Benny Goodman, which is not surprising since the King of Swing has been one of his major influences over the years as has the New Orleans clarinetist Irving Fazola. Some critics have compared him with "Peanuts" Hucko. Allan can be downright blistering as well as warm and mellow, and his clear articulation makes even complicated pieces seem easy. He solos with a light touch and a knack for catchy melodic twists.

His wife Vanessa is also a clarinetist who plays with several Florida musical groups and is the director of the Central Florida Chamber Orchestra. She joined Allan as a special guest on *Ballads, Burners & Blues*, released by Arbors Records in 2004. Allan returned the favor when he recorded the *Look to the Sky* CD with the Central Florida Chamber Orchestra in 2010 that featured original arrangements by Allan and pianist John Sheridan.

He points out on his website, *altissimo-music.com* that his company, "Altissimo Music presents the music that my wife Vanessa and I perform with our friends at festivals, concert halls, clubs and record on compact disc. It is about good music – some of the finest jazz and classical music you will hear anywhere. Even though we could categorize the different types we play, we don't try to group our music into little boxes. We just play good music in a variety of styles we've leaned to love, be it Mozart or Muggsy, or Beethoven or Benny."

JOHNNY VARRO
Has Played with the Best

Published June 2014

There aren't many jazz musicians of note with whom **Johnny Varro** hasn't played during his 61-year career. No pun intended, but when the 84-year-old Varro talks about his career, it's like listing a who's who of jazz greats from the past half-century.

© Dragan Tasic - www.nga.ch

Johnny grew up in Brooklyn and didn't become interested in music until the age of 10. His mother "played a little piano" and gave him a few lesson. Since the family owned a piano, she decided that John should take lessons from a retired concert pianist who lived down the street. "She was a marvelous teacher," Johnny recalls, "and the lessons only cost a dollar a week."

That arrangement continued for several years. Then one day his father brought home two Commodore records, one that featured a trio composed of Jess Stacy, Bud Freeman and George Wettling, and the other by Eddie Condon's band with Joe Bushkin on piano. "I realized I was hearing something totally different from anything I had heard before, and I couldn't get enough of it," he said.

He next was exposed to recordings by Teddy Wilson and Art Tatum as well as several books on the intricacies of playing jazz, which became working tools for Johnny. He would frequent the Commodore Music Shop in Manhattan where he purchased records for $1.03 and met two of the managers, Lou Blum and Jack Crystal, father of comedian Billy Crystal. He soon connected with an older friend who introduced him to musicians like Joe Sullivan, Willie "The Lion" Smith and Bobby Hackett at Central Plaza and Stuyvesant Casino, then located on the Lower East Side.

It wasn't long before John was sitting in on some of these sessions, recalling, "I was half-scared to death, but thrilled to the bone to be associating with these musicians that I had come to admire so greatly. I just kept gigging, learning tunes, trying to improve my style, and above all, listening. Before long, I started to get paid."

He feels his playing ability matured at just the right time to allow him to fit into the jazz activity taking place in New York City, specifically the small band, free-swinging, pick-up group variety. While still in his late teens, he frequently performed at Nick's, Eddie Condon's and Jimmy Ryan's. With the Korean War going on, he was drafted into the Army in 1951 and spent time in the Signal Corps that got him into cryptography along with doing some writing and arranging for camp shows.

Discharged in 1953, he wasn't sure of what he would do in civilian life when he received a call from Bobby Hackett. Bobby had kept track of Johnny through John's father who worked in a drugstore in the RCA Building where the NBC studios were located. Hackett was about to go on tour and invited Johnny to be part of his quartet that included drummer Benjamin "Buzzy" Drootin.

In 1954, Varro worked at Nick's with Phil Napoleon and later with "Pee Wee" Erwin. "We did a lot of things with that band, including appearing live on the Paul Whiteman and Kate Smith television shows." In 1957, Eddie Condon asked him to replace Ralph Sutton as the intermission pianist at his club, and he eventually became the pianist in Condon's band. For the next few years between Condon tours, Johnny could be found performing at the popular jazz joints around New York like The Embers, Roundtable and Metropole. He also appeared with Bobby Hackett on the Steve Allen late night TV show and would play duets with Allen during rehearsals.

In 1965, he moved to Miami Beach, Florida to be part of the warm-up band for the Jackie Gleason "Honeymooners" television show. For the next 14 years, John worked hotel jobs, played with the likes of Napoleon, Flip Phillips and Billy Butterfield and toured with the Dukes of Dixieland. Then came the move to Los Angeles in 1979 where he gigged with Eddie Miller, Dick Cathcart, Tommy Newsome, Red Norvo, Abe Lincoln, Bob Havens and Jack Sheldon and had a five-year solo stint at Gatsby's Restaurant in Brentwood. He returned to Florida in 1993 where he now resides in the Tampa Bay area. He was honored as "Emperor" of the 2003 Sacramento Jubilee.

In the late 1980s, Johnny was an instructor at the Sacramento Traditional Jazz youth camp where it was customary to organize the campers in small groups and have a competition. "The kids I had were terrible and just couldn't play jazz," he said. "So I decided to write simple arrangements. The first two tunes I arranged were *Buddy Bolden's Blues* and *Black & Tan Fantasy*. The kids really caught on and found something where they could solo. We won the best band competition. I think Jason Wanner was a member of that group." Such was the beginning of Varro's Swing 7.

Johnny initially started to write and arrange for his own satisfaction, but virtually all of the 100-plus arrangements he has done over the years have become part of the Johnny Varro book. "Arranging has been an important part of my jazz world," he says. He has lost count of how many recordings that he's been part of on various labels, including many as soloist or leader. The four Swing 7 CDs recorded by Arbors are among his most popular.

It goes without saying that a recounting of Johnny Varro's career involves countless colorful stories. One of his favorites involves the Italian waiters at Condon's back when he was the intermission pianist. "One waiter named Ambrose just destroyed the English language," Johnny chuckled. "One night he came over to Buzzy and I, and said, 'I have a requesta for you to play, *Coma Rain or Comma Shine* – either one'"

When he was in the Condon band, a patron approached the bandstand and requested that the band play *Muskrat Ramble*. The individual made a big deal of reaching into his pocket and placing a 50-dollar bill on an old tom-tom the band used to hold drinks and as an ashtray. As the man walked away, Wild Bill Davison looked at the bill and in a loud voice said, "Just a minute, sir. Would you come back and tell me exactly how you expect us to divide $50 among six musicians?" There was a moment of awkward silence as the patron realized that every eye in the place was on him. He slowly took out his wallet and placed a 10-spot on the drum.

Clarinetist "Pee Wee" Russell had played with the Jean Goldkette Orchestra and Red Nichols, but battled alcoholism the last 30 years of his life. He used to say, "I live on brandy milkshakes, scrambled-egg sandwiches and whiskey." PeeWee would often come to Condon's with his dog – a schnauzer that had a little mustache just like his master – and sit at the end of the bar.

One night he showed up without the dog, which prompted Johnny to ask, "Where's Winky?" to which Pee Wee sadly responded, "I'm mad at him. He let me down." Seems that whenever Pee Wee got a couple bucks ahead, he would stash the money under a rug in the apartment where he and his wife Mary lived. "The last time I hid some money, Winky saw me, and he dug it up and gave it to Mary. We're not talking these days," he lamented.

Johnny acknowledges there were periods in his career when he too battled John Barleycorn, which brought up a story involving another "Pee Wee" whose real first name (like Russell) was Charles. In the mid-1950s, Varro was in a band led by trumpeter "Pee Wee" Erwin that had a four-week engagement at the Grandview Inn in Columbus, Ohio. All went well two weeks into the run when "Pee Wee" was invited to a cookout on his birthday by well-meaning friends who made the mistake of leaving a full bottle of whiskey on the kitchen table, which Erwin proceeded to drain and pass out.

When Erwin didn't show up that evening, Johnny and Kenny Davern went to their hotel looking for him. In the days before air conditioning, there was a 12-foot fan in the lobby which "Pee Wee" had staggered into. Finding him out cold in his room, John remembered, "He was lucky he wasn't decapitated or killed."

Johnny reflected, "It's sad that most of these great musicians are no longer with us, but I feel privileged to have had the opportunity to get to know and play with so many of them. Jazz has been my whole life. I've gotten something from every piano player I've ever heard. I learned long ago that it is important to know the songs, to provide the chords, and to be a team player and not get in the way of the others on the bandstand."

JASON WANNER
Travels the Winding Road to Success

Published December 2013

Jason Wanner's youthful appearance belies his many accomplishments over the past three decades. (He was born on February 1, 1978.) His journey has taken him from his two-finger renditions of Bach's Toccata and Fugue in D Minor or a Scott Joplin rag on his uncle's organ at the age of four to his current status as a highly-respected performer, arranger and teacher.

Growing up in Sacramento, he was exposed to the wide range of music that his parents enjoyed, neither of whom were musicians. What set him on his musical path was an incident in kindergarten when he was told he had "the fingers of a pianist." He excitedly reported this to his parents who asked if he was interested in taking lessons, to which he enthusiastically replied, "Yeah, I wanna play!"

Shortly after his sixth birthday, his parents purchased a Kohler spinet which he still plays today, and the lessons began. His early instructors didn't seem to challenge Jason until Dan Lofing became his long-time mentor. Lofing decided to skip the traditional teaching methods and to proceed directly into classical training.

Jason recalls, "For the first couple years, I refused to learn how to read music because I preferred to play by ear. I was able to do this because I would ask my teacher to play my lessons before I took them home. I could remember what the teacher had played and then figure out the assignment, pretending to be reading the music. However, this didn't work for long because as the pieces grew more difficult, Dan realized I wasn't playing the tune exactly as written. He also taught me that understanding a style meant understanding all of its parts, including those that are more ethereal and not readily apparent."

For the next six years, Jason's focus was on the classics and ragtime. He learned the popular songs of the day on his own, wanting to be like Vince Guaraldi who wrote and popularized the music for the Peanuts cartoon series on television. "I hated practicing, "Jason said. "Those were the longest half-hour and hour-long sessions of my life. I just wanted to play the Charlie Brown stuff all day instead. That's what my friends like to hear me play."

His growing love of jazz was fueled when his Dad took him to his first Sacramento Jubilee at the age of seven where Big Tiny Little became his idol. He joined the Sacramento Ragtime Society and had his first paid gig helping a man sell pianos at a local grocery store. He attended his first Sacramento Youth Jazz Camp at age 12 where legendary pianists Johnny Varro and K.O. Eckland took him under their respective wings. Jason said he began to feel the freedom in his music that he had been seeking, and the foundation of a budding career started to take hold.

In 1993, he hooked up with Stan Mark's New Traditionalists, a jazz combo composed of young musicians that got to perform at the Jubilee. The band eventually evolved into Crushed Red Pepper and later Timeless Tradition. In high school, he played in various orchestras and bands and was the rehearsal pianist for the Spring musical while maintaining good grades.

He next headed off to Los Angeles and the University of Southern California's prestigious music program, which proved to be a bit of a jarring experience. He remembers, "The musicians at USC were absolutely outstanding. I realized that I wasn't the only one doing what I was doing – and they were doing it a whole lot better. That scared me. Plus my scholarships were not being renewed at the end of my freshman year, so I moved back home with my tail between my legs. I just wanted to quit and find something else to do."

While attending the Sacramento jazz camp, he had a chance to jam with the instructors, and at the 1997 Mammoth Jubilee, he got to play with The Professors where Barbara and Tom Hazzard heard him. They invited him to perform at the Sun Valley Jamboree later that year. He told the Hazzards, "Your festival saved my career and turned everything around in my life." He sat in with the Blue Street Jazz Band, and the following February he received a call to join the band in Seaside, Oregon as a replacement for Michael Kaeshammer.

"They were looking for a steady piano player, and it seemed like the perfect fit for me," he said. "As a teenager I said I always wanted to play with this band. When it happened, things really took off, and we were doing as many as 25 festivals a year, plus cruises." He has appeared as an all-star at jazz parties in San Diego and Roswell, New Mexico, and for a time, he held down the piano chair for the Titan Hot 7.

He received a Bachelor of Music in Classical Piano Performance from the University of California-Sacramento in 2007 where he studied under a graduate of the Juilliard School of Music. Jason has been an instructor at the Sacramento Youth Jazz Camp since 1995 and then at the Mammoth Jazz Camp, saying, "I want to give back to those who have done so much for me."

He produced his first CD, *Going My Way*, on his own – all of 10 copies – in 1999, to be followed by *Nature Boy* (2005), a classical album (2007) and *Just You, Just Me* (2010), along with several audio and video recordings with the Blue Street aggregation over the past 15 years.

A resident of San Diego since 2008, he teaches 18-22 year-olds two days a week at a special ed school and periodically will take on private students. He composes and arranges for a variety of shows, films and recordings and occasionally organizes informal sessions of an 11-piece swing band known as Swing Syndicate composed of old friends and youth camp graduates Photography is his spare-time hobby, and his favorite movie – not surprising – is *Amadeus*. He states, "I want to be as versatile as possible and learn something new every day."

Reflecting on his career as he looks to the future, he states, "So far it has been more wonderful than I could have possibly imagined, but I know it will be a difficult road. The world is shrinking due in large extent to the Internet and Social Media. Jazz cannot continue to be just concert music. It has become more functional like it was in the early days. We are developing new audiences, especially dancers. I would like to be involved in giving jazz broader exposure, especially from an educational perspective. Overall, I consider myself to be very lucky. I love playing the piano, but I know I don't want to spend the rest of my life playing in smoky lounges for 40 people every night."

WESLA WHITFIELD
"Time to leave the room"

Published February 2018

(I was introduced to song stylist Wesla Whitfield at the Plush Room, a popular San Francisco cabaret, and immediately joined her legion of admirers who recognized her as one of the most gifted interpreters of the Great American Songbook. I was privileged to see and hear her perform with husband-pianist Mike Greensill at various venues around the country over the ensuing years and to interview her at the 2014 Cleveland Classic Jazz Party. The message she left when she passed away on February 10, 2018 at the age of 70 was "It was time to leave the room.")

Mike Greensill and Wesla Whitfield

Because of her deft rhythmic sense and uncanny ability to connect with the emotional truth of a lyric, the jazz world had no qualms about embracing **Wesla Whitfield** as one of their own. Her approach was intimate; her voice instantly recognizable. She often gave master classes on vocal performance with emphasis on lyric interpretation.

A review of one of her concerts reinforced why Wesla was a favorite of thousands of fans who heard her in person or listened to one of her many recordings. Under the headline, *"This Voice Needs No Adornment,"* the reviewer wrote, "Among the evils *American Idol* has unleashed on the world is the notion that to sing a song, one must perform vocal gymnastics in such a frenzied manner that the actual song becomes all but unrecognizable, not to mention eviscerated of all meaning, soul and heart."

"Wesla Whitfield doesn't do that. She doesn't need to resort to vocal tricks because she has a real voice. She understands that good singing is also good storytelling. Each song is a little novel, something rich with meaning and emotion, and she brings us effortlessly into the experience of the song."

She agreed with the iconic pianist Teddy Wilson, who when asked about his approach to improvisation, said he felt it important to obtain a copy of the original composition so he would know exactly what the composer wanted the tune to sound like as well as the chords he had chosen to get the desired results. Once learning the original, Teddy would adapt to his style, but admitted he generally played the song pretty much as written, feeling there was little he could do to improve the original.

A native Californian and the youngest of three girls, Weslia Edwards (with the added "i" in her given name) acknowledged she knew at the age of two-and-a-half that she would grow up to be a singer. She earned a degree in music from San Francisco State University, and her first job was as a salaried chorister with the San Francisco Opera. She performed at various San Francisco cabarets along the way and also worked as a singing waitress at a restaurant in nearby Burlingame.

On April 12, 1977 following a rehearsal, she was walking back to her car when she was hit in the back by a random .22-caliber bullet that left her paralyzed from the waist down. Two years of arduous physical therapy followed, but in less than three months and confined to a wheelchair, she was back on stage. "There was no way I wasn't going to sing," she recalled. "In the midst of being depressed, I knew I would figure out how to do things. I just went on doing what I had been doing before the accident."

As she fought to regain her health, she worked as a paralegal and computer programmer while rebuilding her singing career. By 1987, she was successful enough to concentrate solely on singing and for a time, opened for Michael Feinstein on his national tours. After teaming up with Mike Greensill, a typical response to their joint appearances was "Every number was framed in a smart arrangement and given its own particular shape, weight and feeling. Wesla knows how to 'talk' a lyric and personalize the story it tells with subtle dramatic and comic touches. In spite of her physical limitations, she delivers a song in an expressive and animated fashion. In short, she is a lyricist's best friend."

She played all the major jazz rooms and concert halls like New York's Algonquin Oak Room and Carnegie Hall and San Francisco's Plush Room, where she appeared for 26 years – even the White House – and garnered numerous national television, radio and media credits. She cited Karrin Allyson, whom *The New York Times* called "a singer with a feline touch and impeccable intonation," as her greatest musical influence. "Karrin is brilliant and takes what I do and elevates it two or three notches," Wesla responded with her usual modesty.

Rosemary Clooney was her favorite singer, Rogers and Hart her favorite songwriters, and *Looking at You* was her favorite song. She religiously practiced a good 20 hours a week, which followed the advice she would give an aspiring singer: "Practice – practice-

practice, and work as much as you can. The key to being a great singer is to refine and nurture a style that doesn't interfere with the song. That's what I try to do. Always do music tastefully."

When Wesla received SFSU's Alumna of the Year Award in 2001, the citation noted, "Wesla Whitfield's story is one of amazing talent, dedication, perseverance and strength. The career that she has built is an inspiration to us all."

Among the tremendous outpouring of thoughts regarding the passing of Wesla Whitfield, the following says it all: "At times like this, words scarcely seem adequate. I wonder if Wesla knew how many people she touched, influenced, helped, inspired and cheered. The world is a sadder and less elegant place without her."

Mike Greensill

Mike Greensill was every bit his wife's partner on stage. His arrangements always mirror her artistic respect for the material while making the familiar somehow seem new again. He graduated from the Leeds College of Music in England in 1972, toured Europe and the Far East and lived in Hong Kong for four years before settling in his adopted home, the City by the Bay. He has written and arranged for symphony orchestras, including the Boston Pops, and is musical director for NPR's *West Coast Live,* that is carried on 90 stations and which he describes as "two hours of fun and conversation." The couple were married in 1986 and moved to St. Helena in Napa Valley in 2006.

Mike has published a tutorial on *Playing for Singers: The Art of Accompaniment for the Jazz or Cabaret Piano Player,* in which he points out that "Music schools graduate many wonderful jazz pianists hoping to be the next Bill Evans or Herbie Hancock. But what they may not realize is that when they enter the professional world, they will likely spend much of their careers accompanying girl singers.

Vocal accompaniment is a skill quite different from that of the jazz soloist."

He continues, "One of the most powerful marriages of the 20th century is the one between jazz and the Great American Songbook. That Golden Age of American Music actually only lasted for 35 years. The reason so many of these standards are still alive and thriving today is because they are treasured by improvising jazz musicians who delight in their melodic and harmonic magic, and the vocal artists who revel in their witty and intelligent lyrics."

THE FAMILY CIRCUS.   By Bil Keane

"There are millions of songs in
there, but you hafta punch
the right keys to get
them out."

OTHER VOICES

What struck me as I edited the profiles in this book was how much great advice was shared that would benefit young, aspiring musicians who might be thinking about making music their life's career.

The musicians who were interviewed candidly discussed their beginnings, development, experiences, philosophies, struggles, and above all, their joys as music makers. My role was strictly as the conduit in letting them reveal in their own words how and why they chose their particular career path and how it impacted their lives.

*For those who may not have read my first book, **JAZZ BEAT Notes on Classic Jazz**, which is available on Amazon as an eBook and paperback, here are some additional thoughts and bits of advice offered by some of the talented musicians profiled in that book.*

"I'm not a goal-oriented person, but music has helped me find my way. Music has its own rewards. I became a band leader, not because I had great aspirations to be one, but because I wanted to know how music works and not what it does for me. Jazz is like public speaking; it works best when you leave spaces. You need to have good fundamentals and understand music theory, be able to make a statement, and draw people into what you are doing. Versatility and commitment are extremely important."

- **Clint Baker**

"I have always been an ambitious person, and the move to New York was the most ambitious thing I've ever done. It's been a huge transition, and the learning curve has been steep but quick. Who knew immigrating to another country and forging an obscure career would be so tricky. The good news is that I've won the friendship lottery and have had amazing people from whom I can draw information and inspiration." - **Bria Skonberg**

"I've learned so much about myself through my music. I've never done anything else. I can't play a tune exactly the way I may have played it in the past. I don't see jazz as 'jazz of the '20s, '30s or '40s.' It's music. For me, the performance is as much about the energy coming off the stage as the energy coming from the audience. After a show, people ask if I am really having that much fun, and I reply, 'You don't know the half of it. It's even more exhilarating than it looks." - **Michael Kaeshammer** .

"It is always fascinating to hear a musician speak in words about the conversation he plays with notes. Classic, Traditional or Dixieland jazz, call it what you will, has its own language and agreed upon format. Listening to a jazz musician speak of their life with that music offers insights into a rarified world that few get to hear verbalized. "
- **Banu Gibson**

"Great music, regardless of style, challenges the mind and inspires the imagination. Music builds individuality and self-confidence as well as an understanding and acceptance of others."

- **Andy Schumm**

"I love playing this music with accomplished musicians and before appreciative audiences. When I play music, I am truly colorblind and am hypnotized by the rhythms, melodies, harmonies and uplifting spirit of jazz. All that matters is that the music swings. Classic Jazz swings. Mainstream or modern jazz swings, just differently." - **Richard Simon**

"I've learned so much from being around older, more experienced musicians who have instilled in me the importance of putting the music first, doing your homework, knowing recordings, concentrating on 'time', developing your own sound, and sticking with it." - **Kevin Dorn**

"I pay attention to my audience. Music is therapeutic and healing, which is why I do so many different types. When I'm seated at the piano, everybody's whim is my command. I take the old and dress it up in a new suit of clothes, and visa versa. My hope is that people who thought they didn't like jazz will say, 'Oh, that's what jazz is!'" – **Yve Evans**

"I've enjoyed busking on street corners with a cadre of musicians in their 20s and 30s where folks of all ages lose their inhibitions and dance to our music. I can tell you from personal experience that there are dozens of clubs and bars in all five boroughs of New York City as well as in New Orleans where jazz is presented every night and is being discovered, enjoyed and re-invented by the under-35 audience. So forget about sitting around in discussion groups. Get out there and enjoy the party!" - - **Ed Polcer**

"We may not be the jazz side of New Orleans, but we're the next field over. There is always an audience out there. You just have to go find them. Our music is a cultural melting pot, and I've got a head full of ideas. As soon as I finish composing one song, I have two or three ideas for the next one. It's still exciting and challenging, and I will continue doing what I'm doing as long as I can be creative and productive." - **Tom Rigney & Flambeau**

"In the music business today, it's one job at a time, and it's a constant struggle to keep the jobs coming in. It's not a job in the regular sense where one is assured of a regular paycheck. We play because we enjoy what we are doing and because we love the music."
                    - **Rose Marie Barr, Uptown Lowdown Jazz Band**

"Why not preserve and present Classic Jazz the way we do for Bach and Beethoven. I want to see a renaissance of this good old music, especially for kids." - **Vince Giordano**

"As a full-time musician for over 30 years, it's easy to get lost amid the trees and lose sight of the forest. We travel a bumpy road, laden with rocks and pits that trip us up and constantly give us cause to ask ourselves what we were thinking the day we decided to make playing music our vocation. But I have since learned that in those stretches of terrain between those bumps in the road, there are plateaus of tremendous beauty that reminds us that in the notes that flow from us and float high above us, there is magic." - **Dan Levinson**

"It's not about being discovered; it's about discovering yourself, about who you are and what you are meant to accomplish in your short time on earth. I've realized that the more you learn, the less you know. I know my calling is music, and I'm proud to be associated with a group of people who are working to keep Classic Jazz alive. There's nothing more rewarding than being able to bring joy to others through music." - **Molly Ryan**

"If I finish learning the piano next
week, THEN can I play
the drums?"

"I like this kind of guitar music—one
thread at a time."

Made in the USA
Columbia, SC
16 June 2020